Style City
LONDON

StyleCity

LONDON

THIRD EDITION

With over 400 color photographs and 7 maps

 Thames & Hudson

Contents

Street Wise

Style Traveller

Series concept and editor: Lucas Dietrich
Research and texts: Phyllis Richardson
Jacket and book design: Grade Design Consultants
Original design concept: The Senate
Maps: Peter Bull

Specially commissioned photography by Ingrid
Rasmussen, Anthony Webb and Francesca Yorke

Except pp. 122–123 courtesy Firmdale Hotels
and p. 145 courtesy Tom Aikens

The **StyleCity** series is a completely independent guide.

Every effort has been made to ensure that the
information in this book is as up-to-date and as
accurate as possible at the time of going to press,
but some details are liable to change.

Second edition published in 2005 in paperback in the
United States of America by Thames & Hudson Inc.,
500 Fifth Avenue, New York, New York 10110

thamesandhudsonusa.com

Third edition 2008

Library of Congress Catalog Card Number 2007905651

ISBN 978-0-500-21022-2

Printed in China by C & C Offset Printing Co Ltd

How to Use This Guide

The book features two principal sections: **Street Wise** and **Style Traveller**.

Street Wise, which is arranged by neighbourhood, features areas that can be covered in a day (and night) on foot and includes a variety of locations – cafés, shops, restaurants, museums, performance spaces, bars – that capture local flavour or are lesser-known destinations.

The establishments in the **Style Traveller** section represent the city's best and most characteristic locations – 'worth a detour' – and feature hotels (**sleep**), restaurants (**eat**), cafés and bars (**drink**), boutiques and shops (**shop**) and getaways (**retreat**).

Each location is shown as a circled number on the relevant neighbourhood map, which is intended to provide a rough idea of location and proximity to major sights and landmarks rather than precise position. Locations in each neighbourhood are presented sequentially by map number. Each entry in the **Style Traveller** has two numbers: the top one refers to the page number of the neighbourhood map on which it appears; the second number is its location.

For example, the visitor might begin by selecting a hotel from the **Style Traveller** section. Upon arrival, **Street Wise** might lead him to the best joint for coffee before guiding him to a house-museum nearby. After lunch he might go to find a special jewelry store listed in the **shop** section. For a memorable dining experience, he might consult his neighbourhood section to find the nearest restaurant cross-referenced to **eat** in Style Traveller.

Street addresses are given in each entry, and complete information – including email and web addresses – is listed in the alphabetical **contact** section. Travel and contact details for the destinations in **retreat** are given at the end of **contact**.

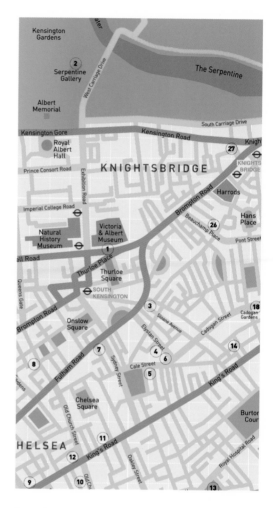

Legend

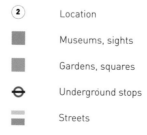

②	Location
	Museums, sights
	Gardens, squares
⊖	Underground stops
	Streets

LONDON

Like many cosmopolises, London is heterogeneous and multilayered, complex and contradictory. According to a 2000 United Nations census, London's greater metropolitan area included around seven and a half million inhabitants, making it the twenty-sixth largest city in the world. Although it may not be one of the globe's top ten most populous cities, it is arguably the most diverse and among the most culturally influential. Bridging the United States and Europe in many, often conflicting, ways and being the capital city on an island has imparted to London a number of curious qualities that have often insulated it from (if not made it resist) the larger continental forces across the Atlantic and the English Channel. Intensified by a dense urban fabric that has been fractured by the Great Fire of 1666 and the Second World War, London's political, cultural and social spheres have a potent way of intersecting and mixing. Unlike many larger European cities, which have grown concentrically out from a historic (usually medieval) centre of power, and most American cities (except Los Angeles), which are based on the democratic grid, London is a concatenation of essentially autonomous villages that have been amalgamated over time. What were once royal hunting grounds in the 17th century or new suburbs in the 19th have been subsumed into the greater whole that is London today.

The result is that London has not one heart but many. With the exception of the Mall, London is unmarked by the grand urban gestures of Pope Sixtus V's Rome, Haussmann's Paris or Cerda's Barcelona, which created axes rather than centres. London's composition of mainly smaller streets and lanes feels distinctly unmodern, unimposing and accessible – a pedestrian paradise. Whereas most visitors regard the main tourist sights – Trafalgar Square, Buckingham Palace, St Paul's Cathedral – as central London, for Londoners there is no true centre, except perhaps the high street of their own neighbourhood. There are financial centres (the City) and cultural magnets (the West End), but in the main London is everywhere. The best way to experience everyday London is in its villages.

The millennium has seen an efflorescence of *grands projets* in the capital, which has revivified the worlds of the arts, design and fashion and substantiated the 'Cool Britannia' image beyond the media. Perhaps the most successful and popular of these recent catalysts is Tate Modern (p. 101), which has awakened the British populace's largely guarded attitude towards contemporary art, provided visitors to the city with a genuinely modern cultural destination, and stimulated a neglected part of London, the South Bank. Moreover, there are less publicized but equally important cultural institutions that are enjoying new leases of life: the intimate National Portrait Gallery has been significantly expanded with a new wing (which includes a restaurant providing unparalleled views over the city; see p. 150). The Royal Festival Hall (p. 102) was refurbished in 2007, and the entire waterfront site, following the Queen's Walk along the river from the County Hall building up to Waterloo Bridge, is being modernized according to a masterplan by Rick Mather. The British Museum, restored to its original 19th-century form, and its Great Court, reinstated under architect Norman Foster's canopy of glass, continue to draw crowds and acclaimed exhibitions. Somerset House (p. 55), too, has been reinvented and restored and its several major art collections brought back to life.

But perhaps no buildings symbolize the city's optimism and 21st-century outlook more than the Greater London Authority building, also by Foster, and the coterie of new glazed structures that now surround it, and the London Eye (p. 100), designed by Julia Barfield and David Marks, on London's South Bank. With their curvilinear forms on prominent riverside positions and their manifest high technology and transparency, they signal London's openness to modernity and new forms of expression. Yet while the face of London may be enjoying a public restoration, the most dynamic element of the city remains its thriving, though less visible underground scene. New trends in music, fashion and art that gain global popularity are often the product of London's subcultures rather than its established institutions. At the turn of the millennium, London images of 'street style' have as much influence on the world as they did in the 1960s. Inspired by an edgy, vital youth culture and the broad spectrum of ethnic influences, London's creative scene continues to confirm the city's position as a world leader.

As with any great city, it is impossible to distil London's essence; even lifelong inhabitants are unable to characterize the city's complexity, to reconcile what is English versus what is international. But London thrives on the very contradictions it creates, the borders that it blurs. Visitors wishing to experience London beyond its tourist destinations will discover its idiosyncrasies, its uniqueness and its timeless appeal in the places that follow. As the city prepares for the 2012 Olympic Games, more development of transportation and facilities will enrich the London experience.

Street Wise

Notting Hill • Holland Park • Kensington • Knightsbridge • Chelsea • Mayfair • Soho • Covent Garden • Marylebone • Fitzrovia • Bloomsbury • Holborn • Clerkenwell • Islington • King's Cross • City • Brick Lane • Shoreditch • South Bank • Southwark • Bermondsey

Notting Hill
Holland Park
Kensington

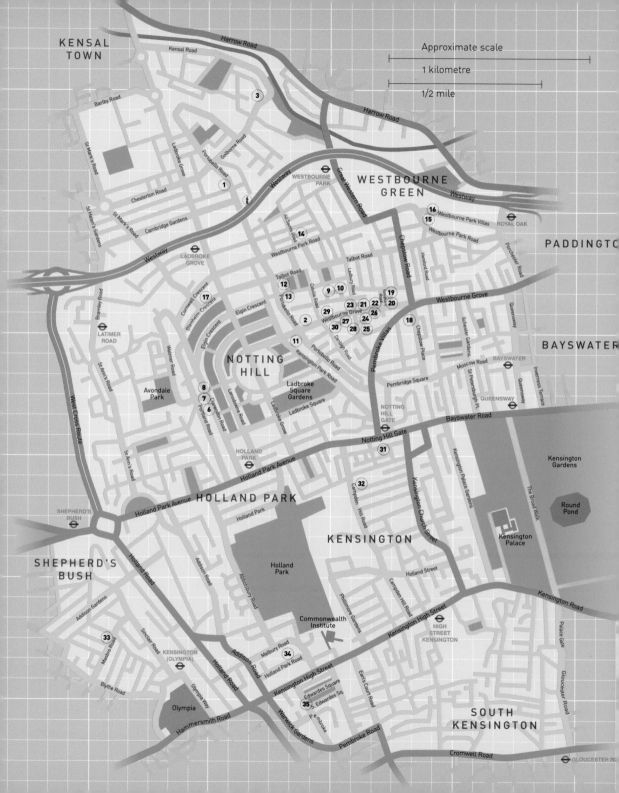

Walking around the designer shops and trendy cafés of Notting Hill today, you would never suspect that as late as the 1950s this was one of London's most impoverished areas, nor would you immediately recognize that it is the centre for the city's Afro-Caribbean culture. The latter distinction is celebrated every August Bank Holiday weekend, when the Notting Hill Carnival swings into gear and around two million people pour into W11 and W2 for days and nights of colourful pageantry, dance music and street-fair fun. When its gentrification began some years ago, Notting Hill became known as the home of 'Trustafarians' (trust fund + Rastafarian), those twenty- and thirty-somethings who emerged from their privileged backgrounds and/or private schools in search of a kind of bohemia, albeit luxurious. So, although gradually regenerated over the past decades and brought into the world's public consciousness by a movie starring Julia Roberts and Hugh Grant, Notting Hill represents a determined effort to preserve the air of an arty-funky lifestyle.

Fortunately for year-round visitors, the atmosphere epitomized by the Notting Hill Carnival can be experienced more than once a year. Every weekend the antiques market on Portobello Road (p. 17), the area's spiritual and geographic backbone, adds a suitable dash of gritty urbanism and multicultural vibe, while providing useful relics of old Victoriana with enough wear and tear to make it obvious they didn't come from the grandparents' manor house. Shops and pubs lining the north end of Portobello Road represent the new blood in Notting Hill in terms of talent and artistic edge. While the area around Portland Road (p. 18) and Clarendon Cross has an air of tranquil luxury, the junction of Westbourne Grove and Needham Road has a more contemporary vibe. The convergence of Westbourne Grove and Ledbury Road (p. 23) is a smorgasbord of designers, galleries and eateries that could easily hold you in their thrall for an afternoon. Famous names and sophisticated newcomers help maintain the area's reputation as a fashion hub bolstered by a clientele of young celebrities and hip, well-heeled socialites.

Farther south, the largely residential and seriously upscale areas of Holland Park and Kensington need little introduction. The quarter's centrepiece is Holland Park itself, providing one of those grand oases of green space in which London rejoices. Whereas so many localities of London are famous – or infamous – for their energy and verve, Kensington is the pure embodiment of English gentility, urban-style. Like so many of the capital's neighbourhoods, it's just another village with a style all its own.

FABRIC HEAVEN

1 The Cloth Shop

290 Portobello Road

Sam Harley and manager Alex Adams have been amassing a treasure trove of new and vintage fabrics in their shop at the top of Portobello Road for over fifteen years. Find antique Welsh and newly made Scottish crofters' blankets, a selection of English wool, Irish linens, and tie silk made in Macclesfield. From further afield they have also sourced twenty hues of Swedish linen and rag rugs, Hungarian fabrics, striped ticking by the metre, and antique mangle cloths from across Europe.

ANTIQUES AND BRIC-À-BRAC

2 Portobello Road

One of London's most popular street markets, Portobello Road has evolved from its late-19th-century association with gypsies' trading horses, and is today known for its stalls of antique furnishings, prints and accessories that attract tourists, collectors and dealers from around the world. The shopping starts to get interesting north of Chepstow Villas. Some of the stalls are offshoots of existing shops, but a good many are independent, with quality varying from real finds to those with more than their fair share of whimsy. The market is also full of clothing, music and a jumble of other items. It's perhaps the carnival atmosphere that is most appealing and only happens on Saturday (though shops are open six days a week). A very pleasant way to pass the morning and perhaps uncover a treasure or two.

VINTAGE STREET

3 Rellik

YOUNG AND INSPIRED

4 Portobello Green Arcade

281 Portobello Road

- Philmore Clague, no. 25
- Natéclo, no. 14
- Baby Ceylon, no. 12
- Sasti, no. 8
- Zarvis, no. 4

Under the cover of the Westway flyover, an arcade of small boutiques with the unlikely appellation of Portobello Green is tucked away off the busy Portobello Road. There is not much green here, but there are plenty of other colours to attract you among the array of young designers.

Philmore Clague is a theatrical designer who turned his attention to women's fashion with near-instant success. Combining figure-hugging waists with bias cuts and crisply draped folds of fabric, he flatters and enshrines the feminine form in a way that has already attracted a celebrity clientele. That same clientele would feel equally at home under the care and attention of Kristy Nguyen, whose diminutive Oriental-style day spa Natéclo offers treatments including steam, essential oils, warm wax mask and massage. Baby Ceylon, at no. 12, was opened by designer Carol McKeown after twenty years of working for other fashion designers. By 2004 demand for her products had prompted a second shop and studio, but here at her first retail space she continues to offer her soft-fitting, sensual dresses and separates, all produced by her studio in London. Makers of 'groovy clothes for kids' since 1995, Julie Brown and Rosie Carpenter of Sasti also manufacture all of their products in the UK. Their fun and funky designs range from zebra-patterned baby bunting to bright logo T-shirts and appliqué jeans. And be prepared to be drawn into Zarvis, where a cornucopia of scented oils, salts and body treatments fragrantly overflows with temptation.

MARKET FASHION

5 Preen

ORGANIC SPA AND A SPOT OF LUNCH

6 Cowshed

119 Portland Road

The original Cowshed is named for the outbuildings it inhabits at the stylish boutique hotel Babington House (p. 180) deep in Somerset. It was here that the proprietors developed their range of organic, vegetarian treatments using herbs from their own garden and essential oils. The London version of Cowshed brings the country spa treatments to the city, or to this villagey area of Notting Hill anyway. Treatment rooms are upstairs in the 19th-century house where tall windows and cushy white furnishings are more comfortable than clinical. The full range of invigorating, exfoliating and/or relaxing face, foot and body treatments are available. The café on the ground floor offers light breakfast and lunch dishes from a changing menu.

Portland Road becomes a villagey collection at Notting Hill's north end, providing a taste of stylish neighbourhood life. Virginia attracts vintage addicts from all over London with its collection of lacy Victorian and latter-day delicates. Its straw hats and flowers are mirrored by the romantic conservatory seating at Julie's across the way, a restaurant that has long been a favourite with the locals and features themed rooms soaked in candlelight by night. Up the road a little farther you'll find another destination beloved of London designers and celebrities: The Cross. As well as carrying new British designer clothing by independent labels like Goat, this boutique sells those little accessories that speak volumes in fashion language.

Daughter of sculptor Henry Moore and trendsetter in her own right, Mary Moore sources and sells top-quality vintage clothing in this little fashion hub on the border of Holland Park and Notting Hill. The word 'collection' very much applies to the select 1950s cocktail dresses, 1960s Hepburn-style coats, and '70s chiffon prints.

Nadia Demetriou Ladas's Notting Hill tableware shop and gallery is the result of an obsession that began when Ladas started collecting 1950s glassware after visiting the glass-blowing region of southern Sweden. Today her commitment to contemporary design is evident in the Scandinavian pieces, Italian art glass, and works by important British designers such as Tom Dixon, Nigel Coates and sculptor Anish Kapoor. 'Everything in the shop has been chosen with passion,' she explains, adding that each piece 'fits into Walter Gropius's definition of good design, that they should have beauty, quality, function and affordability'. These Kensington Park Road premises were designed by Ladas's partner, furniture designer Angel Monzon.

Already a London institution, the Electric has made itself even more popular with a refurbishment by Nick Jones, the man behind Soho House and Babington House (p. 180). An amazing glass frontage conceals a feat of restoration and refinement that has resulted in marvellously comfortable leather armchairs with footstools and tables to hold your movie snacks. There is also an updated bar, open half an hour before screenings. It all adds up to one of the most comfortable and satisfying nights you will ever have at the pictures. Electric Brasserie next door offers formal and casual dining from burgers to fresh seafood: a good place for a post-film chat with friends.

14 The Jacksons
5 All Saints Road

Much-loved English retro-hip designers The Jacksons have a corner shop full of highly coveted shoes, bags, scarves and belts. Their streetwise fashions are featured in other London design shops, but here you can see the whole range. Though the fortunes of All Saints Road have waned, the popularity of The Jacksons has only grown and a second shop selling their own-design shoes is now open on Ledbury Road.

NEIGHBOURHOOD JOINT
15 The Cow

138

THE OUTDOOR LIFE
16 The Westbourne
101 Westbourne Park Villas

The Westbourne is one of those places that looks so inviting and appealing that trying to resist a swift half is futile. Perhaps it's the outdoor terrace, usually filled with youthful locals, or the quiet, tree-lined setting somewhat removed from the area's buzzier streets. A reincarnation of an old neighbourhood boozer, with large forecourt and wood-filled interiors, it boasts a modern menu and attractive clientele that are happy to be in the know.

THE SPICE ROAD
17 Blenheim Crescent
• The Spice Shop, no. 1
• Books for Cooks, no. 4
• Blenheim Books, no. 11

This small street holds a wealth of literary and other surprises. Birgit Erath started with a weekend spice stall on the Portobello Road, and now at the Spice Shop she stocks over 2,500 products and is a source for many a top London chef, who come for her hard-to-find spices and her expert advice. She also dispenses the latter at events held at Books for Cooks, across the road. It's not only a centre for gastro-publishing, but the café in the back also serves well-prepared international dishes, all culled from the tomes on the shelves. However, it's lunchtime only and they don't take bookings. Blenheim Books, at no. 11, is a popular source for books on everything related to the green arts, from planting to landscape design.

LEATHER LUXE
18 Bill Amberg
21–22 Chepstow Corner

If you love leather the way Bill Amberg loves leather, then you will love just about everything he does. His affinity for the stuff means that he doesn't make dainty, strappy accessories, but things that you can run your hand over, have a good sniff of, or walk on. From cowhide floors to vellum for a drawer liner, he expertly works each kind to its advantage. His handbags are ample and luxuriously free of fussy details, as are the modern yet supple cases for men. Attention is given to shape and to the smooth finish, texture and deep colours. The move to these larger premises means a wider range on-site to choose from.

SCENT-SATIONAL
19 Miller Harris
14 Needham Road

Lyn Harris is the young perfumer behind this highly regarded line. After working with perfume-makers in Paris and Grasse, she launched her own range with the help of perfume house Robertet, who helps manufacture her distinctive collection. Basing many of her scents on 'old-fashioned, naturally derived' aromas, she creates such complex concoctions as 'Coeur Fleur', a mix of sweet pea, mimosa, Egyptian jasmine, raspberry, peach, Florentine iris, amber and Madagascan vanilla. The beautifully designed shop also houses her scent garden, 'full of roses, jasmine and herbs', which customers are encouraged to visit. Harris offers a consultancy service, too, inviting clients to access her fragrance library and laboratory to create their own personal fragrances. A second shop is located in Mayfair's Bruton Street.

REDEFINING DECORATIVE ARTS
20 Flow
1–5 Needham Road

Opened in 1999 to 'showcase the best of British contemporary applied arts', Flow was established by Yvonna Demczynska, who had worked as a dealer in British crafts in both the US and Japan. With an interior that is clever but not overwhelming, the work of the gallery's forty represented artists, working in ceramics, glass, wood, textiles, basketry, metal and jewelry, is displayed on floating white shelves. Look out for Kate Allsop's architectural works in porcelain, Amy Cushing's glass tiles using materials developed in the space programme, and nature-inspired metalwork by Kim Harrell.

21 Twenty8Twelve
172 Westbourne Grove

Actress Sienna Miller has put her celebrity pull (and Pepe Jeans owner Carlos Ortega his financial backing) to her sister Savannah's design skills. For her part, Savannah studied fashion design and knitwear at Central St Martin's in London and went on to work for Alexander McQueen (p. 173), Matthew Williamson (p. 47) and Betty Jackson before launching her own label. The results are much more interesting and affordable than we have come to expect from celebrities-turned-'designers'. Here it is the clothes – a bit of artful bohemian,a bit of streetwise flair – that draw your attention, so much so that it is easy to forget the famous people behind them, which seems to be the point of the shop name. Coats and dresses have crisp, flattering pleats as well as a bit of funky detailing, and they certainly have a way with doing a slimmed waistline, never a bad thing.

MAGICAL JEWELRY
22 Solange Azagury-Partridge

NEIGHBOURHOOD CHARM
23 Ledbury Road
- Duchamp, no. 75
- Fiona Knapp, 178A Westbourne Grove
- Caramel, no. 54
- The Ledbury, no. 127

Ledbury Road is a fulcrum of the Notting Hill scene, charming with a parade of small, idiosyncratic shops. Mitchell Jacobs at Duchamp specializes in men's dress shirts, ties, cuff links and socks with decided flair. Jacobs has a real penchant for strong colour, so you will find candy-hued shirts in three different cuff designs (casino, double and two-button) paired with ties full of texture and bright, contrasting colours in modern patterns, as well as geometric, jewel-set cuff links. New Zealand-born Fiona Knapp's blackened jewel box on the corner of Ledbury Road shows off her innovative metal arts in settings like sprays of fireworks or bold, coloured stones set together. Her 'Mosaic' collection was inspired by Byzantine and Baroque churches, while the seductive shop interior dressed in black velvet and amethyst silk took its cue from the film *The Leopard*. Next door, Anya Hindmarch (see p. 37) has a shop selling her signature bags, as well as shoes and other accessories. Lawyer-turned-designer Eva Karayiannis began her children's range, Caramel, by scouting local designers and makers in England and Scotland. Then she turned to designing herself, incorporating 'European style with laid-back Englishness'. Her clothes for children are both robust and stylish, with traditional cuts and fabrics and bright, modern colours and details. Further north along Ledbury Road, a tasteful pub transition has resulted in The Ledbury. Within a lovely chocolate-coloured, minimal décor, inspired dishes such as courgette gazpacho, crab and basil club sandwich, and rabbit lasagne are turned out by chef Brett Graham with aplomb. Definitely worth a detour off the main drag.

CHOCOLATE ARTS
24 Melt
175

COSY KNITWEAR
25 Ross+Bute
57 Ledbury Road

British fashion entrepreneurs Lindy Ross and Serena Bute first gained notice with their colourful thermal camisoles and twinsets. In 2005 they set up this, their first shop, to cater to their growing public demand as well as a list of celebrity clientele that they had already attracted. Simple, feminine separates along with knit dresses and the thermal favourites are all available here. A second shop on the King's Road in Chelsea opened in 2007.

A NEW WORLD OF TEA
26 Tea Palace
148

FOOD AND FASHION CONCEPT
27 202
202 Westbourne Grove

This Nicole Farhi concept store was launched in 2002 and holds a selection of the designer's mens- and womenswear, alongside antiques from around the world and Farhi's own range of home furnishings. The shop is much more inviting and accessible than many such venues, comprising two airy, gallery-style floors. On the ground floor, set amid the beautiful clothing and objects is a homey café serving nicely prepared dishes in a casual-chic atmosphere.

28 Ghost
36 Ledbury Road

Tanya Sarne's floaty creations have been accumulating applause and fashion awards since 1990. Designed, as she says, 'by women for women', they are intended to make every woman feel beautiful. Sarne eschews hard lines, concentrating instead on 'how a fabric feels against the skin'. To that end, her 'vintage-feel' crêpe, velvet and satin, for example, are put through a special production process to achieve their sensuous, flowing quality and to make them surprisingly robust, 'a modern traveller's dream'. The shop in Ledbury Road is her flagship store, and reflects her unique blend of relaxed femininity.

HOME FROM HOME
29 The Main House
128

SOUTH AMERICAN FUSION
30 Wall
1 Denbigh Road

Peruvian Hernan Balcazar and his British-born wife, Judith, have brought the riches of Andean fabrics to London with inventive flair. As creative director, Judith Balcazar works with in-house designers to create women's clothing that is comfortable as daywear and elegant enough for evening. From T-shirts to linen jackets and alpaca coats, the pieces signify 'simplicity, luxury and comfort'. Using blends of hand-picked cotton, alpaca and vicuña, the pieces tend towards neutrals in summer and warm contrasts in winter, such as dark cinnamon and cherry.

GLAMMED-UP OLD FAVOURITE
31 Geale's
2 Farmer Street

The original fish restaurant opened in 1939, and earned a faithful following over the years for its no-nonsense fish and chips. In 2007 the restaurant was polished up and reopened by the Concept Venues team: Mark Fuller, Andy Taylor and executive chef Garry Hollihead. While the black and white interiors have all the clean looks of a new, glamour-infused venue, the trio have vowed to serve 'the best beer-battered fish in town'. They have also added a Champagne bar (which also serves drinks for kids), outdoor seating, and a takeaway and delivery service.

PLEASING DECAY
32 Windsor Castle
154

PLEASANTLY CROWDED
33 The Havelock Tavern
57 Masbro Road

This popular pub restaurant is somewhat off the beaten track, but it shows how consistently good food and a lively atmosphere can maintain a success story. The staff are relaxed, the interior doesn't try too hard, and everything from the steak and chips to the fried monkfish is fresh. Be warned though: fresh food runs out, and they do not accept credit cards.

PRE-RAPHAELITE GESAMTKUNSTWERK
34 Leighton House Museum
12 Holland Park Road

The former studio-house of the high Victorian artist Frederic, Lord Leighton (1830–96) is a spectacular paean to 19th-century decoration and craftsmanship, with an exotic Eastern flavour that was popular among Leighton's artistic circle. Leighton took up residence in 1868 and continued with the embellishment until his death. Among the house's many treasures are perhaps the finest collection of tiles by William de Morgan and a theatrical Arab Hall complete with fountain, elaborate mosaic floor, cupola and stained glass. Leighton's meticulous drawings and some of his paintings, as well as others by contemporaries Edward Burne-Jones, John Everett Millais and George Frederick Watts are in the collection.

AGEING GRACEFULLY
35 The Scarsdale Tavern
23A Edwardes Square

In one of Kensington's most exclusive neighbourhoods, less than a minute from Kensington High Street and filled with bright-white Georgian terraced houses, is an enchanting public house with a façade that looks straight from a chocolate box. No commercial reproduction this – it's an age-old favourite of the well-heeled locals who savour the good food and quiet, homey atmosphere.

Knightsbridge
Chelsea

With the vast, lush green expanse of Hyde Park to the north and the gleaming Chelsea Embankment to the south, the largely residential areas of Chelsea and Knightsbridge are probably the most picturesque and stereotypically preserved areas of London. Chelsea's immaculate terraced houses, dripping with purple wisteria in the summer, and Knightsbridge's high-end shopping create a patch of what can only be described as incredibly civilized London.

The spirit and symbol of Knightsbridge for most visitors is Harrod's, which still holds a certain cachet as a purveyor of luxury and designer-brand goods. For locals, however, it is the smaller, more intensively stylish department store Harvey Nichols, at the top of Sloane Street, which emerged during the 1990s as the vanguard of the younger set whose parents shopped at Harrod's. Rather than providing the feeling of a grand old country-house larder, Harvey Nicks' upstairs food hall is contemporary and sleek.

Harrod's and Harvey Nichols might reflect the tension between tradition and modernity that gives so many parts of London their edginess, but Knightsbridge's creative side is driven by the presence of the Victoria & Albert Museum (p. 30), whose magnificent collections have ensured that the surrounding area has what must be one of the highest concentrations of fabric and upholstery stores, together with interior designers, in the world. Although the character of much of the area's design remains at the traditional end, there are clear signs that attitudes are changing: a new architecture gallery at the V&A and adventurous programming, catalyzed by a team of young curators, offer ever-more exciting exhibitions. Increasing globalization has brought modernity to classic sensibilities in the interior-decoration realm as well — David Collins's Blue Bar (p. 151) is a great example.

Ever since the King's Road made a splash in the 1970s, Chelsea's shops and designers have continued to present their particularly English take on high style and fashion. The shops along Sloane Street are dominated by predictable global fashion labels, so those seeking funkier boutiques and more adventurous outlets should head to the King's and Fulham Roads. But seek out the smaller streets, like antiques-shop-lined Walton Street, Beauchamp Place (p. 38) or the villagey atmosphere of Elizabeth Street (p. 37), because they capture Chelsea's charming character and the quintessence of classical — or modern-traditional — English design more than anywhere else in the capital.

GARDENS OF DELIGHT

1 **Victoria & Albert Museum**

Cromwell Road

The largest museum of applied and decorative arts in the world needs little introduction. You might see only one collection – 'Clothing through History' in the Dress Gallery, for example, or the splendours of the Asian and Islamic Art collection. You might spend a lot of time staring at the Great Bed of Ware in the grand, not-to-be-missed British Galleries (1500–1900) – with pieces by Chippendale, Morris, Mackintosh, Wedgwood and Liberty – or Lord Leighton's frescoes after having visited his astonishing house (p. 25), or the magical Glass Gallery. Whatever you manage to see, no visit should be without a stroll through the Pirelli Garden, an Italian-style piazza garden set within the late-19th-century walled courtyard. A large central fountain gurgles beneath swaying trees: in summer a tented enclosure serves refreshments and visitors can enjoy the garden and museum until 10 pm on Wednesdays.

GALLERY AND GREENERY

2 **Serpentine Gallery**

Kensington Gardens

The largest of the royal parks, Hyde Park's vast green space in the centre of the city contains pockets that each have their own particular beauty: from the classic English Rose Garden and romantic 19th-century statuary and an Italianate folly, to the Diana, Princess of Wales Memorial park (one of London's most imaginative play areas) and Speaker's Corner, a magnet for public soapbox-style debate since 1855. Occupying a former tea house is the Serpentine Gallery, which presents world-class contemporary art exhibitions in a more relaxed setting than the severity of so many of the city's galleries and museums. Most summers an internationally renowned architect is invited to create a folly for the lawns in front of the museum; recent years have seen works by Zaha Hadid, Daniel Libeskind, Oscar Niemeyer and Toyo Ito (shown above).

AL FRESCO OYSTERS AND CHAMPAGNE

3 Bibendum Oyster Bar

Michelin House, 81 Fulham Road

Designer and entrepreneur Terence Conran has been an influential part of the British restaurant scene ever since he opened his Soup Kitchens in the 1950s. Design and food have combined in a number of widely publicized restaurant ventures by the design guru, but one of his earlier – and most lasting – eateries is located in the Art Nouveau Michelin tyre headquarters (architecturally interesting in its own right). While upstairs is the formal Bibendum restaurant, the ground floor features an informal seafood bar and restaurant serving a wide variety of oysters, caviar and *fruits de la mer* in a patio-like setting next to a bright flower stall.

REFINED DINING

4 Tom Aikens

145

AT HOME WITH THE PERFECTIONIST

5 Tom's Kitchen

27 Cale Street

If Gordon Ramsay is the UK chef from hell and Jamie Oliver is the media's over-exposed little darling, then Tom Aikens is the more subtle success story. The two-Michelin-starred chef has followed on from his foray into formal dining (see p. 145) with a more relaxed eating experience, where the name implies less of the complication, and perhaps bodies of staff, than in the first venue. The tall, black frontage here, not far from the original site, recalls the other restaurant's formal presentation, but then leaves some of the mannered approach at the door. The white tile and spare décor may not make you feel like you're sharing a casual kitchen moment with the chef, but they do go some way towards emphasizing the less pricey, more straightforward menu that still sparkles with the appeal of youthful enthusiasm.

6 Neisha Crosland
8 Elystan Street

British designer Neisha Crosland has closed her own-label shop Ginka, sadly, but her inspiration for textiles is still going strong. Having some of her designs chosen for the collections of the V&A (p. 30), Crosland continues to produce exciting new patterns and textures. This showroom in Elystan Street features her signature graphic patterns displayed on fabrics, wallcoverings and paper products.

GLORIOUSLY VINTAGE
7 Butler & Wilson
189 Fulham Road

Simon Wilson has been designing costume jewelry for over thirty years, and some of his better-known pieces are creatures – the 'lazy lizard', 'slinky serpent' and 'friendly spider'. But there are also the delicate drop earrings and pendants in soft pastels, gems that are displayed alongside the shop's array of vintage items, which includes a selection of antique Scottish jewelry, Art Déco pieces in silver, semi-precious stones and marcasite and a treasure trove of one-off bags – beaded, box-shaped and zippered. The retro-looking turquoise-wash exterior makes the shop leap out from the parade of upmarket boutiques on the Fulham Road, promising something inviting and altogether more fun.

SHABBY GENTILITY
8 Anglesea Arms

SHIRT SMART
9 Emmett London
380 King's Road

Robert Emmett started out as a tailor but then became 'dissatisfied with the imperfections of off-the-peg shirts' and began making his own garments 'with discerning taste and tailoring them to the highest standard'. He sources fabrics all over the world and has the shirts made to his designs in Italy. The 400 designs available each season boast details such as contrasting panels under collars and cuffs, and only twenty-five shirts are produced to each design. Choose from double (French) cuffs, single cuffs and casual shirts in unusual patterns and textures; a hint of something tailor-made but not trying too hard to get noticed.

THE FINEST POINT
10 Manolo Blahník
49–51 Old Church Street

Manolo Blahník's gold-accented shop is a must-see for any lover of footwear, with dramatic displays that raise shoes to the level of art objects, and many are just that, as his customers around the world are fully aware (Madonna says they're 'better than sex'). There is a high degree of concept, design and craftsmanship behind each pair of 'Manolos', the last for which the Canary Islands-born designer carves himself. Leathers are dyed in bright contrasting colours like pink and yellow or turquoise and lime. Despite his now firmly established fame, since first being 'discovered' by legendary fashion editor Diana Vreeland in 1970 and more recently brought into public consciousness by *Sex and the City*, Blahník is still the perfectionist who controls every aspect of the design and manufacture, and his first store in Chelsea is the place to find the genuine article.

HISTORIC REPRODUCTIONS
11 William Yeoward Crystal
270 King's Road

British glass designer William Yeoward set up his first sparkling shop on Chelsea's King's Road in 1996 with the ingenious idea of creating reproduction Georgian crystal for purchase off-the-shelf or by special order. Stem- and barware, jugs, decanters, plates and vases are all hand-blown and hand-cut to historic patterns, many in fine floral designs. Yeoward also presents a refreshingly modern take on reproduction tableware. Launching a homeware collection that includes furniture, lighting and accessories, Yeoward moved to these larger premises.

AND SO TO BED
12 Couverture
310 King's Road

Emily Dyson says that her signature is in the detail, rather than in the grand design, and that is what catches the eye at Couverture, a shop originally dedicated to well-designed bedclothes and bed-linens that now features a range of small-label fashions for women and children. Formerly a designer for British fashion leader Paul Smith (see pp. 48 and 166), Dyson still carries a small selection of luxury bed-linens, but has expanded her fashion range to pieces by young French designers April May, 1950s-esque creations by Japanese label Mina Perhonen, and funky traditional British style for kids by Quincy.

A SPECIALIST GARDEN

13 Chelsea Physic Garden

66 Royal Hospital Road

A delicate and unusual green space, the Chelsea Physic Garden was planted as the Apothecarie's Garden in 1673 to educate apprentices in the identification of plants. The riverside setting was chosen for its milder climate, which would support non-native species, and the first greenhouse in England was built here in 1681. Though set away from tourist attractions, the garden is well worth a detour, especially when combined with a walk along the Chelsea Embankment or a look at the nearby Chelsea Royal Hospital, designed by Wren in 1692.

DELHI STAR

14 Rasoi Vineet Bhatia

143

BEAUTY IN THE DETAILS

15 V.V. Rouleaux

54 Sloane Square

'A paradise of *passementerie*' is how Annabel Lewis describes her breathtaking assortment of fine ribbons, bows, tassels and beads. Now V.V. Rouleaux is a single-stop destination for trimmings for clothes, furnishings, just about anything that could do with a flourish or a touch of colour or sparkle. The eye-catching crêpe, organdy and silk ribbons, flowers, braids and countless other irresistible ornaments are all as appealing as wrapped candy.

PRINCE OF SILVER

16 David Mellor

174

GLAMOROUS BAGS

17 Lulu Guinness

3 Ellis Street

Her handbags have animated the pages of *Vogue*, *Cosmopolitan* and *Elle* and adorned the arms of Madonna, Björk and Elizabeth Hurley. But Lulu Guinness is no slave to fashion: she makes fashion all her own. Call them whimsical, naive or cartoonish, but her floral prints, 'house' designs and signature 'flowerpot' bags are instantly recognizable. Colourful, bright and delightful, her shop has irresistible sweetshop appeal. If her designs remind you of 1950s Parisian fashion plates, that's just one example of the old-style glamour that inspires Guinness.

ENGLISH UNDESIGN

18 Eleven Cadogan Gardens

SCANDALOUS LIAISONS

19 Cadogan London

118

THE LIFE OF RILEY

20 Rachel Riley
14 Pont Street

Rachel Riley has taken traditional children's clothes and sweetly refined them with hand tailoring and beautiful fabrics worked in her atelier in France. The results are a nod to the 1950s in crisp cottons and linens, bright polka dots, stripes and custom prints. Riley also has a range of finely crafted clothes for teens and women, and now has a second shop on Marylebone High Street as well as a US flagship store in New York.

NECESSARY ACCESSORIES

21 Anya Hindmarch
157–158 Sloane Street

Anya Hindmarch found her style niche at the age of nineteen, when she discovered the fondness Italian women had for simple drawstring bags. Her designs are colourful, witty and well crafted: photo-print beach scenes look like vintage postcards and beaded mosaic pop-art bags, such as the 'Heinz Baked Beans' bag with a beaded 'label' stitched on to a tin-shaped denim carrier, have become classics. She made headlines beyond the fashion press in 2007 when she created the sustainable shopping bag labelled 'I'm not a plastic bag' in conjunction with an environmental charity. But her focus is still her individual style in upmarket bags and accessories. In late 2007, she closed her original Pont Street shop to open large flagship stores here and in New Bond Street.

QUEEN OF STREETS

22 Elizabeth Street
• Erickson Beamon, no. 38
• Ben de Lisi, no. 40
• Ebury Wine Bar & Restaurant, no. 139

The villagey appeal of Elizabeth Street, tucked between the posh avenues of Chelsea and the less salubrious environs of Victoria Station is an enduring pleasure. Bolstered by the appearance of The Thomas Cubitt (see right), it also offers the delights of shops such as vamp jewelers Karen Erickson

and Vicki Beamon, who create modern baroque pieces that grace the fashion pages and the couture collections of the international fashion set. Their unique boutique will draw even the skeptics in for a closer look. American-born, London-based designer Ben de Lisi also keeps his shopfront premises here, where visitors can see for themselves the flawless lines and inventive fabrics that characterize much of his work. Shoppers in need of refreshment can nip into The Thomas Cubitt or farther along at the corner of Ebury Street, the well-established and much-loved Ebury Wine Bar & Restaurant.

TOP HATS

23 Philip Treacy

STRAIGHT FROM THE CATWALK

24 Tracey Boyd's House
42 Elizabeth Street

Designer Tracey Boyd has lit up the catwalks with her bright, slim-fitting clothes that range from feminine prints to textured linen to jeans and corduroy. Boyd's own-label shop was transformed in 2007 into a designer's personal home-retail space selling not only Boyd's popular ready-to-wear, but also objects and furnishings chosen by the designer as, she says, so many of the things she used previously to decorate her shop were coveted by clients who came in to look at clothes. Alongside furnishings and accessories, all fabrics, beading and embroidery are Boyd's own design.

COSY PUB-CUM-BRASSERIE

25 The Thomas Cubitt
44 Elizabeth Street

The latest addition to the collection of well-heeled shops, galleries and cafés on Elizabeth Street has the origins of an English pub but the light and airy ambience of a European brasserie. The main room with its cosy wood panelling has high ceilings and large windows and tables spilling onto the pavement outside. While the look and feel of the surrounding 18th- and 19th-century architecture has been maintained, along with homage to the builder responsible for the structures that went up around Belgrave Square and Pimlico in the 1820s, the menu goes for a more modern adaptation, especially upstairs where the restaurant proper is located with views overlooking Elizabeth Street. Snacks and traditional ales can be enjoyed casually downstairs, while the upstairs dining room offers a more intimate and formal setting for a more ambitious menu.

STREET OF GOLD

26 Beauchamp Place

- Dower & Hall, no. 60
- The Map House, no. 54
- Groom, no. 49
- Townhouse, no. 31

A street of haute couture and luxury goods, Beauchamp Place also has some quirky and creative things to offer. Jewelers Dower & Hall have long been a fixture here, but their designs have a more youthful appeal than their traditional surroundings would suggest. Sitting somewhat incongruously amid the high fashions is The Map House, a source of antique maps, globes and engravings for almost a century. Groom is a new addition to the street, offering organic products along with a modern range of treatments. Spruce yourself up and cool yourself down in time for a drink at Townhouse, a chic-funky bar and restaurant where you can recline in leather sofas to sip a lemongrass and chilli Martini.

AN EYE FOR FASHION

27 Cutler & Gross

7 and 16 Knightsbridge Green

Opticians Graham Cutler and Tony Gross transformed eyewear from necessity to fashion statement over thirty years ago, inspired by 'the British love of non-conformity'. Their world-renowned designs are available at their original London premises, designed in 1969 by Piers Gough, where they still do eye exams. A second shop at no. 7 sells vintage C&G designs and classics by YSL, Christian Dior and Pucci. With over 600 styles of frames in their archive, you're bound to find something that's you.

HAND-CRAFTED AND SIMPLE

28 Egg

36 Kinnerton Street

Designers Maureen Doherty and Asha Sarabhai create clothing for young and old in relaxed styles that are luxuriously well made in India using traditional weaving and stitching techniques, from designs based on traditional work garments to those inspired by 17th-century Indian menswear. They also have exhibitions of largely British contemporary craftspeople.

FASHIONABLE SCENE

29 Blue Bar

151

egg

Egypt

North
Africa

Mayfair
Soho
Covent Garden

Inevitably and somewhat inexplicably, most visitors to London make their way to Leicester Square, Piccadilly, Regent Street, Covent Garden. In their own way, each of these places represent for many people London's energy, its metropolitan air, its buzz. But stripped of their local colour, over-illuminated by neon, overpopulated by unthinking tourists and often infiltrated by gaudiness, many parts are now little more than symbols of former greatness, their grandeur denuded by the globalizing monoculture. Get quickly away from these magnets and you are in the heart of the West End – dense, chic, lively and ever-changing.

West of John Nash's wonderfully grand boulevard, Regent Street, is Mayfair's dense concentration of high style and fashion, art and commerce. Bisected by Bond Street – lined with a mixture of international fashion labels and classic old shops and galleries – Mayfair is true-blue upmarket London, a genuine oasis of gentility between Piccadilly and Oxford Street. Many of the shops, auction houses and galleries – and therefore also the restaurants and bars – cater to a small group of the wealthy and well heeled, but there are pockets of affordability for all of us. If you've allowed for a one-off extravagance, this is the place to indulge.

Crossing Regent Street going east, you are unmistakably in Soho, flashy and seedy, creative and degenerate, hip and outmoded. The first sign is the once cool, now downmarket Carnaby Street, a resonant reminder of how changes in fashion are accelerated in the city centre – though running parallel one street away, Newburgh Street (p. 51) is alive and well. Although the area's high density of media and creatives maintain Soho's buzz during the day, and recent pedestrianization has made it a generally pleasant place to stroll, its primacy as London's liveliest night spot is slipping eastwards, toward Hoxton Square and Shoreditch. Soho is still buzzing, and, according to Kevin Spacey, director of the Old Vic Theatre (p. 105), 'changes character more frequently than a schizophrenic method actor in a one-man show'.

Since its gentrification in the 1970s, when its old vegetable market was moved south of the river, Covent Garden has attracted a largely youthful crowd with its numerous bars and many designer boutiques selling the latest streetwear. With the refurbishment and expansion of the Royal Opera House, however, an older, more culturally inclined group demanding higher standards of food and drink has had an impact. The Palladian-style piazza, designed by Inigo Jones in 1635, is the quarter's centrepiece and tourist mecca, but the small streets and alleyways that surround it have much to offer – if you know where to look.

GENTLEMANLY GROOMING

1 Geo F. Trumper

9 Curzon Street

While men's grooming habits and styles have wavered over the past century, Trumper's commitment to professional service has not. Still occupying beautiful period premises, the shop that began catering to London gentlemen in 1875 offers a range of services, from haircuts to facial cleanses to chiropody. They even conduct a 'shaving school' where you can learn the best technique to use at home. Trumper's own range of toiletries are on gleaming display in front, while the full menu of treatments, including the ever-popular wet shave with open razor, are performed at the back of the shop by the waistcoat-wearing professionals.

ARCHETYPAL CARVERY

2 The Grill Room

PEACEFUL RESPITE

3 Mount Street Gardens

Off Mount Street

This wonderfully secret, enclosed green space laid out as a public park in the late 19th century is surrounded by grand Queen Anne-style houses and shaded by giant plane trees. In the southeast corner is the Church of the Immaculate Conception (known as the Farm Street Church), built in 1849 and containing an altar by A.W.N. Pugin, architect of the Houses of Parliament.

HIGH-STYLE SEAFOOD

4 Scott's

BRITISH FASHION IN FOCUS

5 Browns + Brown Focus

24–27 and 38–39 South Molton Street

There are many places to buy designer wear in London, but few have the cachet that Browns has achieved over the past four decades. Joan Burstein and husband Sidney opened the shop in 1970, and since then it has become a revered name in London fashion. Browns features well-known designers from all over the world, while Browns Focus, across the street, demonstrates Burstein's prescient eye for young innovators, which is evidenced in the shop's 2001 design by one of Britain's most in-demand architects, David Adjaye.

THE NEW MODERN

6 St Alban

REINVENTING SARTORIAL ELEGANCE

7 Savile Row

THE EPITOME OF STYLE

8 Sketch

140

THE NEW BESPOKE

9 Timothy Everest

35 Bruton Place

British tailor Timothy Everest proudly hails from the headlines of the New Bespoke Movement, creating menswear that demonstrates, by his own description, 'eccentric style and modern attitude'. Yet his bespoke, made-to-measure and ready-to-wear lines still maintain the high levels of quality and craftsmanship associated with the long-established tradition of British suit-makers. He has a star-studded roster of clients, who also come to see him by appointment at his atelier in a restored 18th-century house near Spitalfields Market (see p. 91).

OUTSTANDING SECOND ACT

10 Wild Honey

12 St George Street

In an area dominated by the suit-makers of Savile Row (see p. 165) and their sartorially discerning clientele, the restaurants can assume the stuffy air of an old gentlemen's club, which is one of the reasons that Wild Honey, the younger sibling of the acclaimed Arbutus (p. 137) in Soho, makes such a refreshing find. With its Georgian-style plasterwork dancing merrily above fine oak woodwork, it is both reassuring in its traditional Britishness and exciting in its modernity. Dishes win praise by raising up basic ingredients to high standards of preparation and presentation: pumpkin soup served as a *velouté* to be poured over crisp bread with olive paste; pollack and leeks with fennel purée; razor clams with tiny chopped tomatoes and chilli. And all with a very interesting wine list made even more so by the fact that a number of options can be ordered by the glass or 250ml carafe.

OLD AND RELIABLE

11 The Guinea

30 Bruton Place

This pub, tucked away down a quaint little mews off moneyed Berkeley Square, is a reminder of days past before the looming buildings surrounding the square were built. Dating back to the 15th century, it has a modern restaurant addition that is famous for its classic grills. The small atmospheric bar is loved by high-flying locals and lucky wanderers alike for its Young's brews and award-winning steak-and-kidney pies. If the glittering modernity of Mayfair becomes too much, The Guinea is a welcome old-world refuge from the haute cuisine and couture, but not from high standards.

HIGH-STYLE JAPANESE

12 Umu

132

THE ARTISAN'S ART

13 Rupert Sanderson

33 Bruton Place

Rupert Sanderson has been quietly making waves in the fashion world, being described in *Vogue* as 'years ahead of his generation'. After training at Cordwainers College, and apprenticing at John Lobb (p. 166), he rode a motorbike around Italy visiting shoe factories, and produced collections for Sergio Rossi and Bruno Magli. His lean, sexy designs are available at various outlets worldwide, but this own-label shop opened in 2004. Looking to bring the worlds of fashion and art together, Sanderson wants his premises to have something of the quality of an art gallery about them. To this end, the shop features furnishings from the reclamation specialists Retrouvius, which are for sale. But it is Sanderson's shoes that take centre stage, objects, he says, 'of high craft' such as the dance-hall inspired line for winter 2004.

VENICE VIA MAYFAIR
14 Cecconi's
5A Burlington Gardens

It looks like one of those London restaurants – vaguely Art Déco interior, vaguely Italian name – that could be a mediocre mishmash of intentions. But Cecconi's has a pedigree and level of quality that place it firmly among the capital's top eateries. In 1978 Enzo Cecconi, who ran the Cipriani in Venice, brought fresh pasta, beef carpaccio, tiramisu and Bellinis to the London restaurant scene. Cecconi's was later bought by Nick Jones of Soho House and refurbished under the direction of Ilse Crawford in 2004, who 'brought it back to its Venetian origins'. The only place to serve *cicchetti* (Italian tapas), Cecconi's take pride in presenting simple Italian food prepared to a very high standard. The wine list is an education in regional Italian varieties and the bar is a wonderful cocktail spot.

STAR-QUALITY FASHION
15 Stella McCartney
173

COLOURFUL CHARACTER
16 Matthew Williamson
28 Bruton Street

Nearly next door to fellow British fashion designer Stella McCartney's own designer shop (p. 173), but a world away in terms of style and approach, Matthew Williamson's flagship store is marked by the hot-pink signage on the outside and streaks of bright colour enlivening the cool, white space within. Since launching his debut collection 'Electric Angels' in 1997, which featured bias-cut dresses and separates in tangerine, magenta and fuchsia, he has become known for his sexy, sweeping designs in bold hues. Star clients include Madonna, Sarah Jessica Parker, Gwyneth Paltrow and Kate Moss. The store, which opened in 2004, features ready-to-wear separates as well as products from Williamson's 'lifestyle' range, including candles, the eau de parfum 'Incense' (produced with Lyn Harris; see Miller Harris, p. 20) and his own signature fragrance.

Dover Street and its environs have become something of a mecca for the fashion crown who prefer a little beyond the limelight. The new shop by designer John Rocha expresses all of the glamour and simple elegance of his fashion label. At the doorway, a glittering wall sets off one of his understated designs, and the boutique unfolds to reveal clothes that still demonstrate Rocha's affinity for natural fibres, which first brought him to attention when he was working with Irish linen in his early years as a design graduate. Though he has been based in London for over thirty years, this is his first shop in the city. Across the road, young womenswear designer Effi Samara sits prettily at the corner of Stafford Street. Samara's tailored and flared jackets and skirts have gained a star following that includes Kirsten Dunst, Alicia Keyes and Gwyneth Paltrow. And around the corner the Paul Smith Curiosity Shop is a den of riches, showing off Smith's penchant for the eclectic and his aversion to mundane corporate branding. Furnishings and flea-market finds sit alongside books and fashion. 'Something for everyone (with taste)' would certainly be a good rubric.

As shopping engenders thirst, the perfect stylish quench is to be had in the new Donovan Bar on the ground floor of Brown's Hotel. Named for fashion photographer Terrence Donovan and designed by Olga Polizzi, the bar is a sleek, new modern setting for a collection of his black-and-white photos, including the more risqué selection hung in the 'Naughty Corner', and sophisticated cocktails. Great for glam décor, people-watching or just a civilized drink before the crowds gather.

Of the several arcades built during the early 19th century, the most famous (and longest) is the Burlington Arcade. Today some seventy high-quality shops, many of which are independent, offer a range of clothes, leather goods and jewelry. The smaller Royal Arcade includes Ormonde Jayne (p. 167) and a Martí Guixi-designed Camper store, while Princes and Piccadilly Arcades feature menswear.

THE FRESHEST FISH

27 J. Sheekey

28–32 St Martin's Court

Something of an enigma among the tourist-laden streets of Covent Garden, J. Sheekey has the high-powered provenance of being under the guidance of the founders of Le Caprice and the Ivy, along with a simple approach that puts quality above frills. So while the décor is plainly pleasant, there is a sense of understated glamour here, as the clientele include theatre producers, directors and actors. More importantly, this just might be the freshest seafood to be served in central London. And whether you go for caviar and lobster, scallops and black pudding, fish cakes or fish and chips, it's doubtful you'll be disappointed.

MODERN COUNTRY STYLE

28 The Haymarket Hotel

122

A BOTTLE OF THE GOOD STUFF

29 The Vintage House

42 Old Compton Street

The worn blue awning of The Vintage House shields a veritable *Wunderkammer* of malt whisky, worth a pilgrimage for the connoisseur. On rows of boxed shelves, wines, other liquors and cigars share space with sought-after whiskies. Malts from every region and age include special bottlings and collector's decanters. If the thought of lugging a bottle back on the plane seems too risky, you'll just have to drink it before you leave.

DIM SUM AND THEN SOME

30 Yauatcha

141

TEA WITH A VIEW

31 The Portrait Restaurant

150

The maze of small, mostly pedestrianized streets behind Regent Street holds everything from chain boutiques to street-market chic. The Dispensary sells a range of street-style designer labels; across the way is Jess James, offering jewelry by young makers. At no. 5, Cinch features a high-tech-looking premises originally by Dutch design collective Droog.

A romantic old favourite offering cosy respite from the clamour of Soho bars and clubs, Andrew Edmonds serves traditional English cuisine that is consistently well prepared in an atmosphere that's always welcoming.

This small, unpub-like bar is a Soho standby. Though it serves beer only by the half-pint, encouraging the consumption of wine instead, it is often too crowded to move your elbows in the late-week evenings and amicably full the rest of the time. Legend has it that this was a hangout of London members of the French resistance and, sitting as it does surrounded by traditional old pubs and trendy new cafés, it retains the aura of stubborn pride, much like its home country. Delightfully shabby, it has more character in one scratched wine glass than most of the new places put together. The upstairs restaurant is intimate and off-beat, but the food varies with the chef.

Who better to re-create classic British clothes with a modern street-smart twist than a Japanese company dedicated to 'New-Brit style'. With the number of Japanese designers dominating the fashion scene, and with the country's reputed fondness for traditional British goods, it is perhaps not surprising that the firm Abahouse has focused on remaking English favourites. The corduroy jacket, the great coat, the Macintosh – they're all here, together with a slightly more tailored line, subtle detailing, and luxurious fabrics. With the likes of Jude Law and Ewan McGregor as regular customers, Designworks looks to be setting a few trends of its own.

There are many jazz venues in London, but Ronnie Scott's attracts the biggest international talents. Scott, himself a saxophonist, opened his first club in 1959 and in 1981 was recognized by the Queen for his 'services to jazz'. The much-loved but increasingly decrepit venue was bought in 2005 by Sally Greene, who also purchased and revamped the Old Vic Theatre (p. 105), and given a makeover by the popular French designer Jacques Garcia. There is a proper menu served from a proper kitchen these days, and a private members' club upstairs. Prices have gone up, but so have the acts; recent headliners have included Chick Corea, David Sanborn and Wynton Marsalis.

Rokit started trading among the Bohemian streets of Camden in 1982. Now the growing taste for vintage amongst those who like their shops tidy and the merchandise pressed rather than stacked in rumpled piles has brought Rokit into the big time. With shops opened in Brick Lane and Brighton, and fashion stylists from the likes of *iD*, *Dazed & Confused* and the *Sun* newspaper plundering their racks for photo shoots, you will still find that vintage prom dress, Hawaiian print or 1950s gabardine shirt, as well as classic army-issue items and nearly new denim all looking crisp, and at prices more down-to-earth than you might think.

There is more poetry to this little café, the haunt of the London Poetry Society, than just the parchment-style lampshades with inked verses scrawled across them. By day it's a pleasant but unassuming little café – away from the madding crowd coursing through Covent Garden's nearby pedestrian zones – where light and inexpensive vegetarian lunches are served. At night it becomes the venue for poetry readings, workshops and music. Tuesday nights feature open-mike poetry; on Saturday evenings, it's poetry and jazz.

After studying at the National College of Art in Dublin and the Royal College in London, Irish-born Orla Kiely blossomed onto the fashion circuit in the early 1990s. Going against the grain of fashion that was 'black and conceptual', her bold prints were soon the ones to spot around town. She is now one of the top design names in Britain and has produced commissions for museums as well as larger retailers. Her women's ready-to-wear, accessories and luggage are available here at her flagship store, which hums with her brilliant patterns.

46 **Seven Dials**

- Coco de Mer, 23 Monmouth Street
- Monmouth Coffee House, 27 Monmouth Street
- Koh Samui, 65–67 Monmouth Street
- Neal's Yard Remedies, 15 Neal's Yard
- Neal's Yard Dairy, 17 Short's Gardens
- Magma, 8 Earlham Street

This small quarter of narrow, cobblestoned streets, radiating from the the circular intersection of seven medieval roads, and quirky boutiques has become one of London's most hip shopping areas. A short walk along Short's Gardens takes you to Neal Street, a parade of shops that specialize in weird and wonderful shoes, from trainers and rock-climbing slippers to patent-leather stilettos. Monmouth Street, running north from Seven Dials, and Upper St Martin's Lane, running south, are pockets of design-label boutiques. Coco de Mer, the brainchild of Sam Roddick, daughter of the late Body Shop entrepreneur and fair-trade pioneer Anita, offers high-fashion lingerie and erotica. Continuing along the east side of the street, you can stop at the Monmouth Coffee House for a cup of freshly ground dark stuff before heading to Koh Samui, which features a well-chosen selection of top new labels. Neal's Yard, sandwiched between Monmouth Street and Short's Gardens, and entered by way of small alleys, is a centre for organic eating and holistic treatments – Neal's Yard Remedies sells tonics, creams, oils and aromatherapy ingredients, all bottled in the distinctive old-style blue glass. Just outside the courtyard, Neal's Yard Dairy is full of gorgeously pungent cheese. Magma is London's leading store for graphics, design and architecture publications, from local rags to obscure imports.

THE NEW CLASSIC
47 **Paul Smith**
 166

JAPANESE DICKENSIANA
48 **The Old Curiosity Shop**
13–14 Portsmouth Street

Behind the 1567 façade of the well-preserved and well-signposted building that was the model for Dickens' fictional locale is a somewhat surprising real-life reuse. Japanese shoe designer Daita Kimura, who originally occupied the premises with his workshop, has opened the doors to the curious public once again, showcasing his hand-made and bespoke shoes. Having worked for Alexander McQueen (p. 173) and for the trendy Buddhahood design label, Kimura is no stranger to high fashion, but both his own creations and his quaint historic premises suggest something unique, if rather fairytale-like. The shop also sells shoes by British designer George Cox and select, equally unusual European brands.

CULTURAL REAWAKENING
49 **Somerset House**
Strand
- Courtauld Institute of Art
- The Admiralty

With an ambitious plan of refurbishment that began in 1997, Somerset House, one of England's finest 18th-century buildings and formerly the offices of the Inland Revenue, is now home to several art galleries, a fine restaurant, terrace dining, and lively courtyard fountains designed by architects Jeremy Dixon and Edward Jones. Samuel Courtauld's vast personal collection of Old Master and Impressionist paintings was moved here in 1990 and are displayed over three floors. The Gilbert collection of European gold and silver and the Hermitage Rooms are also open for public viewing. Dine in the funky-clubby Admiralty (the name is a reference to the naval offices that used to be based here), established by restaurateur Oliver Peyton (see Inn the Park; p. 149). While the décor, by architect Andrew Martin and designer Solange Azagury-Partridge (p. 171), is an intriguing mix of traditional and modern British, the food is regional French. Outside, the Riverside Terrace has reopened after over 100 years of neglect, and you can enjoy a drink or a meal beneath flowering umbrellas overlooking the Thames. In winter, the courtyard is taken over by an outdoor ice rink.

QUIET AND CLUBBY
50 **Adam Street**
 135

DRIPPING WITH HISTORY
51 **Gordon's Wine Bar**
 151

BUCOLIC BANQUET
52 **Inn the Park**
 149

INDIAN NIGHTS
53 **Cinnamon Club**
 139

Marylebone
Fitzrovia
Bloomsbury
Holborn

Marylebone, the area defined roughly by Oxford Street in the south and the Euston and Marylebone Roads in the north, is a curious mixture of Edwardian proportions, commercial enterprise, apartment living and discreet stylishness. At the western edge is Marylebone High Street, which, somewhat to the dismay of its loyal inhabitants, has in recent years become one of London's premier gastronomic destinations, with a supporting cast of high-quality shops and design stores. Not far in distance but worlds away from the nearby tourist trap of Madame Tussaud's is Chiltern Street (p. 61), a little-known thoroughfare with a quirky collection of fine shops. Farther north, past Marylebone Road, is Church Street and Alfie's antiques market, home to a host of antiques dealers well off the beaten track.

Fitzrovia, to the east, is a maze of small and one-way streets inhabited by advertising agencies (like M&C Saatchi), engineers (Ove Arup, Büro Happold) and furniture showrooms, making it a hotbed of high design. It gets its name from lovely Fitzroy Square, designed on two sides by the neoclassicist Adam brothers in the 1790s. The quarter also has older creative associations, but more of the starving-artist sort. Atmospheric pubs that were once the haunts of humble writers (T.S. Eliot drank at the Fitzroy Tavern, for example) and artists retain their shabby chic, while others have cleaned house entirely, in favour of cutting-edge media houses and restaurants with seductive interiors by top designers that give night-time pursuits an infusion of glamour.

Moving east again, on the other side of Tottenham Court Road, the London moderns take hold in the form of the Bloomsbury set, who made this area the centre of literary modernism. Home to University College London, the British Museum and, until the late 1990s, the British Library (now in a Scandinavian-inspired building on the Euston Road), Bloomsbury retains the aura of a literary and academic enclave, despite the tourist buses that wend their way through the narrow streets. Pleasing squares provide refuge for and reminders of the area's continuing intellectual pursuits.

John Milton, Francis Bacon and Charles Dickens, as well as Dickens's character Pip of *Great Expectations*, all lived for a time in the place known as Holborn, a somewhat transitional area between the old London of the City and the later developments west. The Inns of Court are located here, with their fine buildings and lush enclosed green spaces, as is the former journalists' mecca, Fleet Street, and the wide avenue of the Strand. The best of Holborn is in the isolated historic gems: London's oldest Catholic church and its neighbouring tavern (p. 152), an eccentric architect's historic house-museum (p. 67) and the underground vaults now used by dealers in silver (p. 65).

Chiltern Street is a delightful row of quirky shopfronts with a curious orientation towards wedding fashion and musicians (many of the latter come from the Royal Academy of Music nearby). For the groom-to-be, Gary Anderson creates bespoke suits and formalwear and has a second shop in Savile Row, while musicians should stop in at Howarth the woodwind specialists and the London Harpsichord Centre. Shoe designer Caroline Groves makes shoes by commission and her clients include celebrities, businesswomen and members of the royal family. Next door, Philip Somerville hats add the final touch to the wedding-wear available in the neighbouring boutiques.

Marylebone High Street has a surprisingly pleasant village atmosphere, but Daunt Books would be enough to lure travellers here even without the surrounding shops and cafés. There are many who consider its Edwardian rooms London's most beautiful bookshop. The *pièce de résistance* in both character and design is its foreign section, which features not only guides and maps but histories, fiction and cookery titles – all helpfully arranged by country.

The Wallace Collection is a privately amassed assembly of art bequeathed to the nation by the widow of Sir Richard Wallace in 1897. Among the treasures housed in the grand period rooms of this townhouse are a renowned collection of French 18th-century pictures, porcelain and furniture, some fine 17th-century paintings, and a rather intriguing armoury. A superb glassed atrium was added in the 2000 renovation and expansion, designed by Rick Mather, and provides an ideal place for lunch, tea or a glass of wine.

5 **Mint**

70 Wigmore Street

Mint is 'ethnic, tribal, old and new, solid and pure, hand-made ordinary everyday objects presented as extraordinary', according to shop-owner Lina Kalafani. This wilfully 'eclectic' range of furnishings, textiles and accessories is arranged over two floors of a former wine store and cellar. Next to an old Tibetan chest you might find a piece by Henry Harris, or a pair of felt slippers among the glassware, ceramics and pots.

NO FLOUNCES HERE

6 **Margaret Howell**

163

PUBLIC HOUSE PLEASANTRIES

7 **Dover Castle**

43 Weymouth Mews

This Georgian pub, tucked down a mews in a quarter of mainly private and ambassadorial residences – and just a stone's throw from the RIBA headquarters (see below) – is the perfect place to settle in for a pint. Whether you choose to admire the 1777 interior and wood-panelled dining room, or to join those who spill out into the mews, you will be among the people who live and work here, in a setting visited by few others.

PEERS OF ARCHITECTURE

8 **Royal Institute of British Architects**

66 Portland Place

RIBA is housed in a grand 1930s building that includes galleries, meeting rooms and a world-class architecture bookshop. With 30,000 members, it is one of the most influential architecture bodies in the world. Regular exhibitions, lectures and events highlight new architecture from around the globe. The contemporary first-floor café, remodelled by the Conran group, buzzes with figures from the architecture community and the nearby embassies and consulates lining Portland Place.

FRENCH CAFÉ

9 **Villandry**

170 Great Portland Street

Despite their distinctly French affiliations, which includes produce delivered from Paris, the delicatessen and restaurant at Villandry have become something of a Fitzrovia institution. The food shop is a mainstay of many in search of gourmet ingredients, and the dining room boasts rustic French recipes executed with authentic rigour. Should you find yourself in Regent's Park or near Oxford Street, it is a perfect place for a daytime drink or coffee, or a light lunch featuring nicely accented dishes like pan-fried cod and a great wine list.

SUPERIOR MIXES

10 **The Social**

157

SPOILED FOR GOURMET CHOICE

11 **Charlotte Street**

- Fino, no. 33
- Pied à Terre, no. 34
- Passione, no. 10
- Bam-Bou, 1 Percy Street
- Rasa Samudra, no. 5

This Fitzrovian throughway has become a hub of high-style international cuisine. Choose from a fine selection of modern tapas-style dishes at Fino or consistently well-prepared haute French cuisine that has earned Shane Osborne two Michelin starts at Pied à Terre. Updated and upmarket Italian fare is always on offer at Passione, where chef-proprietor Gennaro Contaldo serves the classics with quality. For French-Vietnamese fusion, Bam-Bou continues to please with spicy additions to traditional dishes. Upstairs, the Lotus Rooms offer cocktails in an elegant Vietnamese atmosphere. Chef Das Sreedharan has made Indian seafood an art at Rasa Samudra, where fish, curry and chilli combinations are pleasantly inventive.

GRILL AND SPIRITS

12 **Roka**

37 Charlotte Street

Partner to Zuma in Knightsbridge, Roka has at its heart the *robata* grill used for a Japanese cuisine that involves searing and roasting portions of beef, chicken, pork, fish and vegetables. Seats at the bar are first come, first served, but tables in the dining area can be reserved. In the more intimate Shochu Lounge downstairs, dark wood and soft chairs and banquettes upholstered in perky Japanese prints provide a sultry atmosphere for sipping *shochu*, a vodka-like drink that comes in a variety of flavours (such as lemon, plum and strawberry) and is served as an aperitif in rippled glasses. Sushi, sashimi, salads, tempura, rice and noodle dishes are all constructed with just the right amount and range of ingredients.

Comte

Cow's milk
The salt is strong but balanced and
the flavour has a nutty tang
£19.50 / Kg

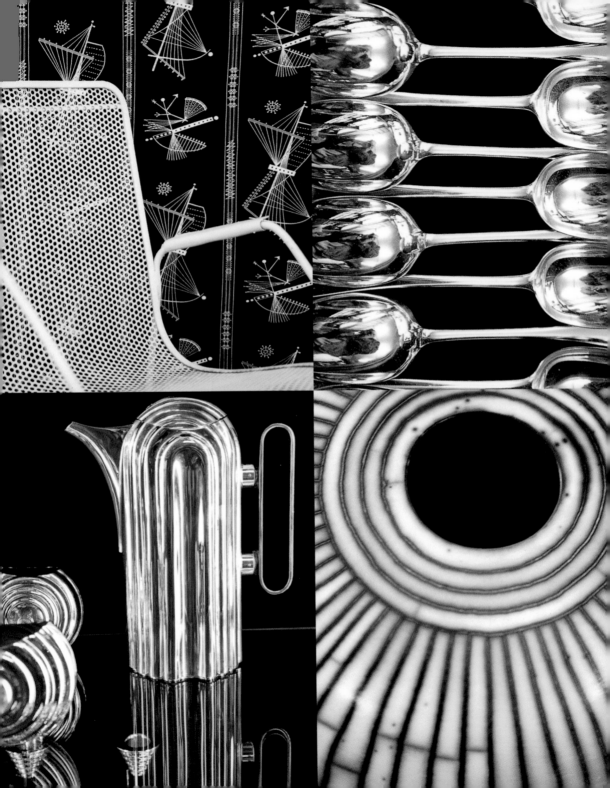

BRITISH MODERN
13 Target Gallery
7 Windmill Street

This unassuming gallery off Goodge Street near Tottenham Court Road has been quietly gaining a reputation for its collection of Modernist furniture, ceramics, textiles and glass. The focus is on British makers such as Robin Day, Frank Guille, William Plunkett and John and Sylvia Reid, but there is also a selection of Italian, Scandinavian and French designers, graphics and Pop Art posters, jewelry by Anton Michelsen, Georg Jensen and Hans Hansen, and a host of other items from the 1930s to the 1970s.

BRITISH ARTS AND CRAFTS
14 Contemporary Applied Arts
2 Percy Street

Founded in 1948 in the spirit of the turn-of-the-century Arts and Crafts movement, Contemporary Applied Arts is the largest private gallery in Britain for contemporary crafts, with a large regular stock and exhibitions of all media: fine and costume jewelry, metalwork, ceramics, wood, textiles, furniture, glass, bookbinding and paper. Works can be bought on-site or commissioned from the hundreds of makers on their books.

EASTERN BEAUTY
15 Hakkasan

LITERARY LIGHTS
16 London Review Bookshop
14 Bury Place

Despite the great literary traditions that have emanated from Bloomsbury's intellectual and cultural centres of University College London and the British Museum, there wasn't a decent independent modern bookshop – until this extension of the *London Review of Books* opened in 2003. Following the dictum 'If a book is interesting, it will find a place on the shelves', it has a 20,000-volume stock, and hosts literary talks, poetry, author readings and debates.

SECRETED SILVERWARE
17 London Silver Vaults
53–64 Chancery Lane

The world's largest collection of antique silver is housed in thirty-seven shops beneath a plain building in what were once the strongrooms for the safe deposit of valuables for wealthy Londoners. From 1867, the vaults were guarded night and day, as they are today, and there has never been a robbery. Since 1953, the vaults have been occupied by dealers, and it has been *the* place to find silver at near dealers' prices. Even if you don't require any Georgian silver plate or Victorian candlesticks, a descent into this quirky arcade is well worth the trip – few locals even know of its existence.

ANOINTED PUB
18 Ye Olde Mitre Tavern

SMALL SENSATION
19 Ragam
57 Cleveland Street

Before all the plaudits, this was just a neighbourhood Indian restaurant with tattered décor and great food. But then a few column-writing foodies were dragged in by enthusiastic friends who told them about the fantastic dishes and the less grand prices, and the queues started forming. This is still a great little place, focusing on the cuisine of Kerala, in southwest India. Some of the mainstays are *utthappam*, a flatbread served with toppings (sort of like a pizza), and *dosai*, flat pancake creations that are filled with wonderful vegetarian and meat mixtures. Even the more familiar *biryani* and curry dishes are all well worth the wait.

WILD NIGHT
20 Crazy Bear

FIRST FOR DESIGN
21 Thorsten van Elten
22 Warren Street

Looking through the design and style pages of many leading journals, one name stands out. Thorsten van Elten, furniture and design enthusiast began working with young British designers to create new products in 2002; first among his contributors were Alexander Taylor, Ed Carpenter and Sam Johnson. He continued to gather new talent and present their work at the 100% Design fair in London and the Milan furniture fair, and eventually opened his own shop in 2004. His reputation for spotting and helping to produce inventive new design continues to grow. This is the place to find pieces by his stable of creators, as well as a range of international designers for whom he is the sole UK distributor.

22 L. Cornelissen & Son

105 Great Russell Street

It looks like an old apothecary's shop with black-painted wood drawers holding all sorts of interesting titbits, and antique cabinetry stuffed with paint pots and tubes, brushes, papers and other specialist artists' necessities. Established in 1855, L. Cornelissen & Son have acquired an international reputation as 'artists' colourmen' that provided them with a busy mail-order business long before the Internet made their stock available worldwide in 2004. However, a visit to the traditional Victorian-era shop, which Cornelissen acquired in 1980, is an altogether more fascinating experience than scrolling through their products online. Here, a stone's throw from the British Museum, professionals and amateurs convene, looking for rare pigments, special varieties of gum, books of gold leaf or one of the thousands of shades of pastel. The more specialized the request, the better the staff like to fill it.

23 James Smith & Sons

55 New Oxford Street

The exterior of this shop makes such a wonderful backdrop for photographs that too many people forget to go inside. Yet James Smith & Sons really is the ultimate in umbrellas and walking sticks. The first Smith set up shop in 1830 and his son moved the business to these premises in 1857, which has been maintained ever since by the Smith family. With the same fittings specially created for it by its own Victorian craftsmen, this was the first company to make use of the Fox steel frame, which distinguishes the Smith & Sons umbrella as the finest in the sky. The company continues to produce walking sticks, though they may be more at home in the country than in the city. Umbrellas range from those created for ceremonial purposes to the everyday, in either solid sombre tones or explosions of vivid colour, and all are working symbols of an era of fine workmanship – and a necessary London accessory.

SIR JOHN SOANE
MUSEUM
Open Tuesday-Saturday
10AM~5PM
(9pm on the first Tuesday
of the month)
ADMISSION FREE
Groups must book in advance
TEL: 0171-405-2107
Lecture tour on Saturday 2:30
Tickets £3. limited to 22

AN INDOOR FOLLY

24 Sir John Soane's Museum

13 Lincoln's Inn Fields

Sir John Soane (1753–1837) was a distinguished architect (most notably of the Bank of England) and art and artefact collector. During his lifetime he amassed antiquities, archaeological fragments, architectural prints and Old Master drawings. The house was completed in 1824, and upon his death in 1837 Soane bequeathed the house and its contents to trustees with the mandate that it be preserved in its original condition. A visit to the Soane, a jewel-box of delights and surprises, is a trip into one man's obsessions and love. If that weren't enough, there are paintings by Canaletto, Turner and Reynolds, and two series by Hogarth. A particular treat is the first Tuesday of each month, when the museum is open in the evening and rooms are lit with candles.

PUBLIC-HOUSE MODERNE

25 The Duke

7 Roger Street

The 1940s are alive and well in this hidden little pub down a narrow street off Gray's Inn Road. You'll certainly need to know it's there, but once you do, you'll be drawn in by the warm mustard-yellow walls, the red lacquered piano in the corner, the changing selection of pictures. The back lounge bar is the most captivating, with wood-backed banquettes that give it the feeling of an old railway café or speakeasy. Pubs of genuine interest from periods after the Victorian age are rare in London, so this pre-modern pub has a slightly off-beat ambience, though the choice of beers and fresh, modern cuisine will appeal to most.

King's Cross
Islington
Clerkenwell

The areas north of Smithfield (or 'smooth field' as it was once known) – Clerkenwell, Islington and King's Cross – amply demonstrate how new life and vitality can emerge out of a dense urban fabric. On the border of the City, acting as a kind of fulcrum between it and its lively northern neighbours, is the church of St Bartholomew the Great (p. 80), which stands proud amid all the surrounding redevelopment. Smithfield Market, a place for cattle- and horse-trading since the Middle Ages (today still a meat market), signals a modern transition with nightclub-goers herding into the Victorian warehouse buildings-turned-dance venues.

Conversions continue in Clerkenwell, to the north, a district once known for its light industrial buildings and lively printing presses, many of which have become stylish lofts. Animated by journalists from *The Guardian* newspaper and a number of internationally renowned architectural figures, such as Zaha Hadid, Clerkenwell embodies that typical London alchemy in which the old world and new ideas fuse into something exciting and unexpected.

Islington, northward again, is another area of successful regeneration. In the 19th century it was one of London's first suburbs, with some of the most unusual and intimate residential squares. Its central-fringe location made it attractive to artists, writers and City bankers, who poured in during the 1970s to refurbish and restore neglected buildings. Today it is one of the most lively and creative of London's villages and still marked by patrician elegance. And although Upper Street (p. 74), the neighbourhood's main thoroughfare, is lined by chain stores, street markets such as Camden Passage (p. 77), independent boutiques and bars ensure the area maintains its street-style. Islington is also enlivened by the highest density of theatres in London, making it a popular stomping ground for thespians and theatre mavens.

King's Cross, which was known until very recently as just a train station, is now considered a neighbourhood in its own right. The arrival of the high-speed rail link to Paris (a mere two-and-a-half-hour ride away) has spawned numerous loft developments coinciding with a profusion of groovy bars and shops. Some people have appreciated the neighbourhood's off-beat feel for years: arch-minimalist John Pawson and design wunderkind Thomas Heatherwick (see Konstam; p. 73) have their studios here, as do the corporate-branding gurus at Wolff Olins. Even though these areas are just outside the ring of tourist attractions (but within an easy walk of the British Library), they have a strong local character that is enriched by the creative and literary people who live there.

GLORY DAYS OF RAIL TRAVEL

1 St Pancras Station

Pancras Road

Now home to the Eurostar, which runs between London and Paris, the train station and red-brick Gothic Revival Midland Grand Hotel (completed 1873–76 to designs by Sir George Gilbert Scott) has finally had the refurbishment that preservation-minded Londoners have been waiting years to see. The translucent train shed itself was the largest space ever enclosed by a spanned structure. The brick building, once a hotel, is now home to loft-style apartments and hotel accommodation by Marriott. But the real draw is the restored Victorian train shed and extension which, true to the advertisements, does indeed bring back some of the glory days of train travel. A large and varied range of chain stores have been opened in the underground arches, but there is also something on offer for the less retail-minded: the longest Champagne bar in Europe, 90 metres of bubbly *joie de vivre*.

LOCAL HERO

2 Konstam

2 Acton Street

If the turquoise floors and furniture don't make you stop and stare, the draped swags of silver beads hanging from the ceiling will. With all the visual enticements of an art installation, created by designer Thomas Heatherwick, Konstam might not have to work so hard at capturing attention with their menu. However, chef Oliver Rowe already established his intentions with his earlier Konstam café, a few doors down from this, his first proper restaurant venture. Rowe came to prominence in the BBC2 series *The Urban Chef*, which followed his search 'to bring locally sourced, seasonal food from all around Greater London to the heart of King's Cross'. He remains true to his word, getting meat from Amersham, poultry from Kent, and even wine from UK growers. The proof is in the pudding, as they say, and Rowe shows that local and seasonal can really be exceptional.

ECO-FRIENDLY EATERY

3 Acorn House

69 Swinton Street

The elegant typescript logo, matching green-themed interior with modern fittings and sharply styled edges have all the hallmarks of a 'concept' restaurant that may or may not deliver where it really counts. Actually, Acorn House takes their concept even further, being an 'eco-friendly training restaurant' that not only strives to be kind to the environment, but to put something back into the community by providing opportunities for local young people to take part in their noble enterprise and gain some valuable skills (and qualifications) at the same time. In this unloved corner near King's Cross a stylish eatery couldn't be more welcome, but restaurant manager Jamie Grainger-Smith and head chef Arthur Potts have aimed higher with both their menu and service, and so far they haven't missed the mark. Fresh modern British dishes and a good wine list all offered at reasonable prices have kept a steady stream of nearby office workers and some destination foodies coming through the doors.

WINE IN TRANSIT

4 Smithy's

153

RED-LIGHT ZONE

5 Ruby Lounge

157

BEER GARDEN REDUX

6 The Albion

155

ACTORS' FAVOURITE

7 Almeida Theatre

Almeida Street

Since it opened as a performance venue in 1980, the Almeida has become one of the most highly regarded small theatres in London. It formed its own producing company in 1990 under the joint directorship of actors Ian McDiarmid and Jonathan Kent, who quickly became known as the man who brought Hollywood to Islington. A-list talents such as Claire Bloom, Ralph Fiennes, Juliet Binoche and Kevin Spacey (now director of the Old Vic Theatre; p. 105) helped the theatre to earn dozens of awards. In 2002 Michael Attenborough was named artistic director, and the refurbished and modernized 1837 building reopened in 2003 with a full programme, set to please both the public and actors alike.

8 Upper Street

- The King's Head, no. 115
- Twentytwentyone, no. 274
- Gill Wing Shops, nos 182, 190, 194, 196
- Euphorium Bakery, no. 202
- Stephen Einhorn, no. 210

Despite its over-commercialization, the exceptional aspects that have made Islington a local and international destination – theatres, crafts, antiques, restaurants – are still thriving at points along Upper Street. At the south end is antiques destination Camden Passage (p. 77). The King's Head is an old favourite, a pub-cum-theatre that features everything from solo performances to vaudeville and Irish music. High-design modern furniture and domestic objects are at Twentytwentyone (and their showroom off Amwell Street), while the family of Gill Wing shops sells cookery items, shoes, quirky accessories and gadgets, menswear and craft-based jewelry. The Euphorium Bakery delights with gourmet bread and pastries. For new Gothic silverworks, Stephen Einhorn produces a whole range of jewelry for men and women.

BOUTIQUE HEAVEN
9 Cross Street

- Fandango, no. 50
- Canal, no. 42
- Cross Street Gallery, no. 40

A small lane lined with Georgian townhouses between Essex Road and Upper Street and filled with independent shops and boutiques, Cross Street makes a pleasant detour from the crowds. Fandango offers unexpected mid-century modern treats like 'Sputnik' hanging lamps and Arne Jacobsen chairs, while Canal, with its finely woven scarves, shawls, jackets and other textiles made in India to designs conceived in-house, is a visual and textural delight. At no. 40 is the Cross Street Gallery, a small space specializing in contemporary paintings and prints by artists such as Bridget Riley.

ITALIAN FUTURISTS
10 Estorick Collection
39A Canonbury Square

Eric Estorick was an American writer and sociologist who lived in England after the Second World War and, together with his wife Salome Dessau, started collecting 20th-century art. Their lively collection has been featured in museum exhibitions since the 1950s, but only found its permanent home in a restored Georgian manor off picturesque Canonbury Square in 1998. The collection focuses on Italian Futurist works and figurative art dating from 1890 to the 1950s. Giacomo Balla, Umberto Boccioni, Carlo Carrà, Gino Severini, Luigi Russolo and Ardengo Soffici are all represented, as are de Chirico, Modigliani, Giorgio Morandi, Mario Sironi and Marino Marini. The small museum also has an art library, café and bookshop.

QUEEN OF SHOPS
11 Handmade & Found
109 Essex Road

Anthony Wilson and Ruth Llewellyn source and design smart, well-made, original womenswear. This shop opened as Comfort & Joy in 2000 and has attracted a loyal clientele. In 2007 it featured in the BBC television programme *Mary, Queen of Shops*, receiving a makeover and a name change under the expert guidance of fashion legend Mary Portas. Featuring Llewellyn's slightly retro designs in eye-catching fabrics, along with a range of local designers, Handmade & Found offers one-offs or very limited runs of shirts, dresses, trousers and skirts at prices that are not far off what you would pay for factory-produced merchandise. Definitely a destination for those with an eye for fashion discoveries.

EDGE CONDITIONS
12 Essex Road

- The Old Queen's Head, no. 44
- Get Stuffed, no. 105
- S&M Café, nos 4–6

Where Upper Street has largely been taken over by large chains, Essex Road running very close by represents the edgier, funkier side of affluent Islington. Historic Essex Road is found in The Old Queen's Head, originally Elizabethan, torn down in 1829 and rebuilt with its original 16th-century plaster ceiling and chimneypiece intact. It's recently been renovated and revved up with club-night gigs. A quirky favourite is Get Stuffed, a taxidermy shop where you can buy a stuffed lion, wolf, peacock, kangaroo, or just about any other animal, as well as the glass case to keep it in. Sausages and mash are English comfort food and the 1950s-style diner S&M is all about a comfortable nostalgia, from the chrome detailing and bright blue formica table tops to the simple menu and Coke in a bottle. Choose from a variety of sausages, from S&M's own mix to vegetarian versions, served with a choice of gravies and sides (mushy peas, bubble and squeak), but leave room for home-made pudding.

THE GOOD LIFE STYLE
13 Palette London
21 Canonbury Lane

Palette London, dominated by vintage clothing, is the brainchild of Marco Ellis, who adheres to his rule that 'if an item is gorgeous, unusual or superbly designed', whether vintage or modern, he'll consider adding it to his collection. Mint-condition designer clothing from the 1920s through to the 1980s, including gems by Christian Lacroix, Emilio Pucci, Oscar de la Renta and Comme des Garçons, as well as furniture, accessories by Unto This Last (p. 88), organic bath products and wallpaper are among the mix of vintage and contemporary treasures.

CIVILIZED DRINKING
14 Islington Pubs
- The Crown, 116 Cloudesley Road
- The Draper's Arms, 44 Barnsbury Street
- Duke of Cambridge, 30 St Peter's Street
- The Marquess Tavern, 32 Canonbury Street
- The Charles Lamb, 16 Elia Street

Established several years ago on a quiet street in the heart of the Barnsbury conservation area, The Crown can be relied upon for pleasant food and atmosphere, a clever selection of wines, Hoegaarden blond beer and Czech pilsner Staaropramen on tap. The Draper's Arms has been winning accolades from London pundits and Michelin critics alike for its menu; popularity from the locals comes from the very comfortably, slightly upscale atmosphere that's just as good for a pint as for a bottle of wine. Meanwhile, in genteel Canonbury, revamped corner pub the Duke of Cambridge continues to attract organic foodies from all over the city, and the fortunes of the Victorian free-standing Marquess Tavern have been revived by the group behind trendy Brick Lane tequila bar Green & Red, who took the interior back to its best bare bones and made a lovely, ever-so-slightly formal dining room in the rear with high ceiling, candles and a hearty traditional British menu. Back toward the Angel tube station, tucked away on a quiet side street, The Charles Lamb is a welcoming neighbourhood-style pub with potted cabbages on the tables, old favourites on tap, and good food on offer.

PINTS IN THE PASSAGE
15 The Elk in the Woods

156

ANTIQUES EMPIRE
16 Camden Passage
Off Upper Street
- The Mall, 359 Upper Street
- Frederick's, no. 106
- Annie's, no. 12
- Tadema Gallery, 10 Charlton Place
- Susy Harper, no. 35

Revived from the doldrums in the 1960s, Camden Passage is a hive of antiquarian activity on Wednesdays and Saturdays that is almost hidden from shoppers in busy Upper Street. The Mall is full of tiny spaces selling everything from antique tiaras and tea services to Art Déco ceramics and wooden sailing ships. Frederick's is an Islington institution featuring a large conservatory and post-hunting luxuries like lobster and beef, and look for Annie's vintage clothing shop, filled with beaded flapper dresses and lacy Victorian linens. Tadema has immaculate Art Nouveau, Jugendstil and Arts and Crafts jewelry. Breezy, blousy women's designer Susy Harper, who moved here from Cross Street, is among a new wave of independent creatives moving into the area. And be sure to check out the overflowing stalls of Pierrepont Row.

RETURN OF AN OLD FAVOURITE
17 Fish Shop on St John Street
360–362 St John Street

The Fish Shop serves fish and shellfish fresh for the day from Billingsgate Market in mostly unadulterated forms that leave the creativity in the chef's selection. The standard battered plaice, cod and haddock are still on the menu, as are things like Cornish crab (served half or whole), rock oysters, fresh langoustines and native lobster. The focus is on the variety of fresh fish simply pan-fried, seared or cooked in batter (or egg and matzo).

DANCE ELECTRIC
18 Sadler's Wells
Rosebery Avenue

On the site of a well believed to have medicinal properties, Thomas Sadler built a 'musick' house in 1683 to provide entertainment for the many visitors looking to take the cure, and there has been some kind of theatre on the site ever since. Today Sadler's Wells is primarily a theatre of modern dance, presenting an international and highly regarded programme. The present building, completed in 1998, has a modern appeal, as well as three bars, a café and exhibition area.

Harriet Wallace-Jones and Emma Sewell have been weaving together since 1990, and in 2003 the pair opened their own shop. Textured weaves in silk, cashmere and mohair for winter and silk, crepe and linen for summer are individual works of art, as the hand-crafted approach endures from conception through dyeing to the detailing.

Their eccentric, intricate and somewhat gothic designs are credited with starting the recent revolution in wallpaper, and now the Scottish duo behind Timorous Beasties have a London showroom where their graphic patterns in brooding colours can be had on fabric and window shades.

Though the paper napkins and plain menu suggest a certain humility, the dishes, prepared by chef Charles Fontaine, are upwardly mobile and cater to bankers and locals alike. Classic dishes from jellied eels to grilled lobster are served in a classic setting of high-backed settle benches. It's not luxurious, but it is quality.

Just a short walk behind Sadler's Wells (p. 77) sits a haven for English-made pottery, presided over by former dancer with the Royal Ballet Gary Grant. Here you'll find a fine selection of famous Rye pottery, as well as new works by Grant, a trained ceramist, and other new designers.

On Monday mornings market stalls sell woven bags, gourmet sausages, cheeses, olives, oils. But every other day this semi-pedestrianized street is brimming with new establishments sitting next to the few remaining local shops. Jeremy Brill combines his love of indie and hard-to-find music with the need for coffee in his warm and welcoming coffee and CD shop, Clerkenwell Music. Moro caused a spicy sensation when it opened, and continues to please with its inspired North African dishes and Spanish tapas, served by Sam and Sam Clark. Medcalf (occupying the former butcher's shop), with its dark, rustic-chic interior, serves hearty dishes with French overtones that are reliably good. The downstairs Martini Lounge at $ Grills & Martinis is an experience in kitschy bling and well-mixed cocktails. For the craft connoisseur, EC One sells jewelry from over forty mostly British designers, as well as a range of bespoke wedding and engagement rings designed by partner and goldsmith Jos Skeates. Japanese-born Takako Copeland and her husband, Matthew, decided to set up Family Tree with a group of friends who considered themselves a 'family' of designers. Takako mans the store that displays her own, hand-crafted jewelry made up of precious metals, semi-precious stones and Swarovski crystals. However, the jewelry competes for attention with hand-made shoes, belts and scarves that all have a distinctly bespoke quality. So, too, do the soaps and tiny boxes for 'transporting valuable insects'.

THE ORIGINAL GASTROPUB

24 The Eagle

138

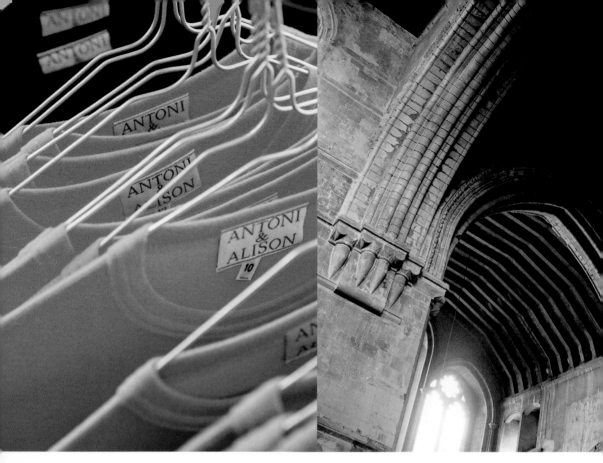

Known for their quirky and wry photographic-print T-shirts and whimsical accessories, Antoni Burakowski and Alison Roberts gained notoriety with their refreshingly humorous catwalk shows. Now their energy and bravado have been channelled into creating a full-blown collection of street-savvy ready-to-wear pieces, including knitwear, dresses, skirts and trousers. They now offer a rather eccentric tour of 'The House of Mr and Mrs Antoni and Alison' as well as their continually evolving collection in the ground-floor shop.

In a lovely preserved corner of narrow streets just across from Smithfield Market is this often overlooked church, the only vestige of the priory founded along with St Bartholomew's Hospital in 1123. Sections of the church have been rebuilt (the Lady Chapel in 1336, the central tower in 1628), and it fell into disrepair until it was restored in the 19th century. Today the church is a tranquil oasis, a little illumination of medieval London.

Clerkenwell has become a mecca for young designers of all media and gradually also yielded to patches of gentrification. At the heart of the revitalization is Clerkenwell Green, a pleasant Georgian square landmarked by the spire of St James's Church, which features shops selling brilliant original creations: the Lesley Craze Gallery has established itself as a showcase for new designs in precious jewelry and carries pieces by over 100 British-based artists. There are also textiles and woven creations by local artisans. For an antidote to any shopping extravagances, visit the Marx Memorial Library, home to waves of revolutionaries, with a subscription library specializing in socialist literature that was opened in response to the Nazi book-burnings.

Smiths sits facing the old cattle market and if you were expecting beef then you won't be disappointed. John Torode (formerly of Quaglino's and Mezzo, and now hosting the BBC's *MasterChef*) has embraced traditional British food and spruced it up with Thai and Italian touches. He began by sourcing rare and organic breeds in Britain for his meat and poultry dishes, and he buys organic produce whenever possible. The venue, a former meatpacking warehouse, is historic, with a large ground floor filled with refectory tables that serves breakfast all day long. On the first floor is a red-leather-boothed cocktail bar to lubricate the way to the second-floor dining room, an informal seated service. The Top Floor is the showpiece for Torode's rare and organic breed dishes: Gloucester Old Spot pork fillet with bok choi, crab ravioli and Thai broth; or Welsh black sirloin, aged twenty-six days.

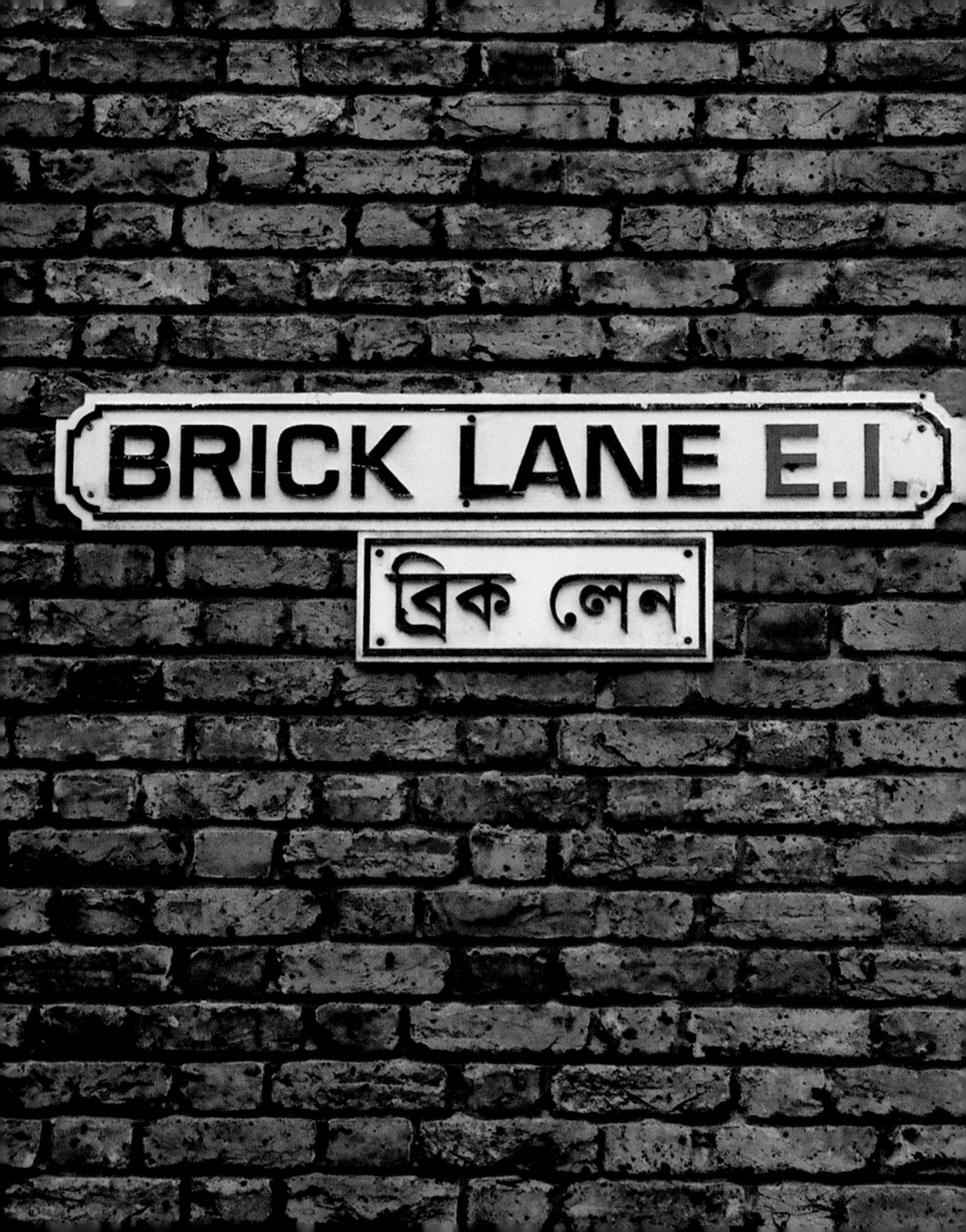
BRICK LANE E.I.
ব্রিক লেন

City
Brick Lane
Shoreditch

Old London, the Square Mile, the City – all refer to the original settled area on the Thames, once ruled by the Romans and now largely known as the financial district, but still imbued with the mystique of the ages. The 11th-century Tower of London was William the Conqueror's declaration of triumph; St Paul's Cathedral a signal of rebirth after the Great Plague of 1665 and the Great Fire of 1666, and a symbol of strength during the Second World War. The City is rife with history and the characters of history – Spenser and Chaucer were born here and Shakespeare flourished here. Nowhere is the fabric of history more tangible than in the architecture – the oldest, smallest, quirkiest streets (matched by public houses that have stood for centuries) are set off by the span of bridges and the profusion of early 18th-century churches. Massive rebuilding after 1945 wasn't particularly design-conscious, but new life has come to the old city, and buildings once threatened with demolition are being saved by the revitalization of historic marketplaces.

One of the most successful centres of civic rejuvenation is north of the City in the area known as Shoreditch. Once a wasteland of disused light industrial buildings, it has progressed from arty bohemian village to almost upscale status. Artists still occupy many of the loft spaces, as do galleries and design-label boutiques featuring local talent. Its artistic profile is heightened by the presence of the White Cube gallery (p. 94) on Hoxton Square (see p. 159), which has lost much of its edginess but not its edge. If you're looking for innovation in music, art and fashion before it gets to the high street, it probably starts here.

Farther east, amid the cacophony of sights and smells that is the East End, Brick Lane (p. 88), where the rag trade, Indian restaurants and odd design experiments converge, is attracting its fair share of creatives. This was once a track used as a route for transporting tiles and bricks during the rebuilding of London after the Great Fire. Spitalfields was an early home to nonconformists, later a Jewish ghetto, and then, beginning in the 1960s, a community of largely Bangladeshi immigrants. The area was steeped in their culture, and Brick Lane became synonymous with home-style curry. But change continues, and both the creative industries and the cuisine have experienced injections of new talent and innovation. The Old Truman Brewery complex (see p. 88) has become a centre for fashion and design, while young entrepreneurs have elevated the curry house from its humble origins. On the weekends, Brick Lane has a lively atmosphere, with wonderful food and one-off boutiques.

CHRISTOPHER WREN CHURCH

1   St Stephen Walbrook

39 Walbrook

There has been a church on this site since before 1096; the previous one, having been built in 1439, burned down in the Great Fire of 1666. Christopher Wren, architect of St Paul's, rebuilt the current St Stephen in 1679 using some methods he would later employ in the great cathedral, including the large central dome, described by one observer as 'a bubble of light'. Although damaged by bombing during the Second World War, it retains its 17th-century features, such as the communion rails, pulpit and font, making for a fascinating glimpse into the mind and career of one of London's greatest architects.

CHAMPAGNE AT THE TOP

2   Vertigo42

150

MODERN ART, ETC

3   Whitechapel Art Gallery

80–82 Whitechapel High Street

With its commitment to show fine works by known and new international and British artists, the Whitechapel Art Gallery is one of London's premier art venues, housed in a soaring Arts and Crafts building, designed by Charles Harrison Townsend, off the beaten path in a gritty area of London near the southern end of Brick Lane. Established in 1901 to 'bring great art to the people of the East End of London', the Whitechapel lists exhibitions devoted to Picasso, Mark Rothko and Jackson Pollock among its early shows. More recently international contemporary artists Nan Goldin, Mark Wallinger and Carl Andre have held exhibitions in the space.

ART NOUVEAU PUB

4   The Blackfriar

153

SIMPLY OLD SCHOOL

5 Sweetings

39 Queen Victoria Street

Sweetings has been going strong in this spot in pretty near the same fashion since 1889. In 2007 it was bought by its former head chef and one of its fish suppliers, a move that ensures the quality and continuity of its offerings. The draw here, apart from the visual and atmospheric nostalgia, is the fresh fish prepared and served with the least frills or fussiness, with the focus fixed firmly on the substance of the dish. Waiters in white jackets have mostly been on the premises for decades, as have a lot of the clientele. As it's only open from 11:30 until 3 pm and they don't do reservations, waiting in line for a table is also a part of the tradition.

BUDGET LUXURY

6 The Hoxton Urban Lodge

112

PERIOD DRAMA

7 Dennis Severs' House

18 Folgate Street

California artist Dennis Severs fell in love with Spitalfields and its history, but his stunning re-creation of early 18th-century life in a London townhouse is an experience unlike any historic or museum study. Severs lived in the house, which he saved from dereliction, with all the trappings of the period, and until his death in 1999 personally escorted guests and visitors around the house in a complete sensory experience. Using everything from period furnishings and art, clothes, utensils and food, he aimed to 'bombard your senses'. 'I will get the 20th century out of your eyes, ears and everything,' he said. The house remains open to occasional tours, and each one is like a journey into an Old Master painting. Meandering silently through the candlelit rooms during evening tours, you are transported far beyond historical reconstruction.

8 New Tayyabs

83–89 Fieldgate Street

There's nothing trendy or stylish about this place, except perhaps the people queueing up (and there will be a queue). Waiters whiz by with steaming, simmering selections of some of the most flavourful and affordable food available anywhere in London. New Tayyabs offers cuisine native to Pakistan, which includes a number of grilled platters as well as curries, kebabs and stewed dishes, none of which are designed to be either flashy or dumbed down for a European palate. You would do just as well to ask for the same thing your neighbour is having as picking your way through the menu to find something familiar. The only caveat, at such low prices, is the tendency to over order. (NB: closed during Ramadan).

MODERN GEMS

9 Ben Day

18 Hanbury Street

After sixteen years as a jeweler in London and Los Angeles, Ben Day has settled in his native city, founding his atelier and shop space in the old Huguenot quarter of London. Noted as a true artisan with his pieces making frequent appearances in the fashion press, Day works with coloured gems, pearls and precious metals to produce jewelry of chunky simplicity, and was recently invited to join Selfridge's new men's brand. His shop is also a glittering little gem.

WHERE CURRY MEETS CUTTING EDGE

10 Brick Lane

- Tatty Devine, no. 236
- Unto This Last, no. 230
- @ Work, no. 156
- Boiler House, no. 152
- Brick Lane Beigel Bake, no. 159
- Le Taj, no. 96

A street long associated with its Asian inhabitants, concentration of ethnic restaurants and the lively Sunday market that fills the lane with stalls and bargain-hunters, Brick Lane has become a centre of cutting-edge art and design. Starting from the north (above Bethnal Green Road) is Tatty Devine, selling avant-garde jewelry, T-shirts and art from its brick-red shopfront. A few doors down, Paris-born Olivier Geoffroy has set up furniture shop Unto This Last in a former pub to sell his beautifully formed birch-ply tables, chairs, bookshelves and room

accessories. Crossing Bethnal Green Road you enter the area of Brick Lane proper: stop by @Work for innovative and uninhibited jewelry designs. Across the lane and slightly south an unmarked door leads to the vast club space that is the Boiler House, a converted warehouse that hosts a variety of club nights, exhibitions and a relaxed café. After clubbing, head for the 24-hour Brick Lane Beigel Bake, but be prepared to stand in a queue and shout your order. Past the Old Truman Brewery (see below) and the art space opposite, the realm of Indian and Bangladeshi restaurants begins. The trend for clean, spare design with modernized ethnic food is heralded by Le Taj, which features an excellent and innovative menu.

ARTISTIC EXPRESSIONS

11 Dray Walk

- Café 1001, no. 1
- Junky, no. 12
- Vibe Bar, 91 Brick Lane

The Old Truman Brewery complex in Brick Lane is now host to exhibitions of up-and-coming young artists, and is identifiable by the bridge over the road (at about its midpoint). A small walkway that is today a shop-lined pedestrian area, Dray Walk is heralded by the bright-orange Café 1001, a good place to stop for a toasted focaccia sandwich, a fruit smoothie or coffee. Further down are exhibition spaces, and shops selling funky T-shirts and trainers. Junky offers 'recycled' clothes: new fashion-designer wear that has been bought as overstock and completely reinvented – a man's suit jacket becomes a woman's halter, a pinstriped suit becomes a pair of 'magic trousers' and lovely 'patchwork' skirts. Look out for the celebrity buyers' who've already caught on. Meanwhile, Vibe Bar's dance-tinged music remains a solid favourite.

REAL MUSIC

12 Rough·Trade

East Dray Walk

Expanding from cramped but much-loved premises in Notting Hill, the new 5,000 square-foot East End shop just off Brick Lane continues the Rough Trade ethos of giving people the best access to and choice of new music. The new premises include a small café area selling coffee, cold drinks and snacks, a performance stage, exhibition space, and 'snug' Internet/workshop corner. It replaces the Neal's Yard basement, which is being taken over by the Slam City skateshop, although they say that the ceiling signed by visiting bands, like Sonic Youth, is still intact.

13 Cheshire Street
- Ella Doran, no. 46
- Dragana Perisic, no. 30
- Mar Mar, no. 16

Cheshire Street began its renaissance a few years ago as little bursts of creative energy on the outskirts of Brick Lane. Now the street has some of the most vibrant new talent in the capital. Ella Doran imbues a range of products, such as tablemats, roller blinds and stationery, with artistic flair using her photographic print designs, and has created a range of designs for the Tate (see p. 101). She is the director of CIDA, which supports the development of the creative sector of London's East End. Whether fitted, smocked or draped, Dragana Perisic's designs have something of a 1940s sharpness and elegance about them. The Yugoslavia-born designer says she came to London to find a motorcycle part and stayed on to attend the London College of Fashion. One gets the sense that this rather discreet and lovely shop may soon be replaced by something grander as her popularity grows. Mar Mar stocks a tasteful and somewhat eccentric selection of homewares from the UK and Europe: a fantastic range of vinyl wall stickers, ceramic birds' 'nesting balls', winged bicycle clips for trouser legs, amongst other useful items.

SIMPLE AND RELIABLE
14 Labour and Wait
18 Cheshire Street

Rachel Wythe-Moran and Simon Watkins were already working together when they discovered a shared 'passion for good, functional, honest products'. In their premises near the market district of Brick Lane, they stock an array of such items of 'classic, timeless' quality. There is a certain Zen-like utilitarian beauty about most of the things they sell, from wooden pencil boxes and rope products to enamelware and watering cans. They now also have a concession in Dover Street Market (p. 162)

FROM VEGETABLES TO VINTAGE
15 Spitalfields Market
Commercial Street
- The Square Pie Company, 16 Horner Square

One of London's liveliest and most varied markets, old Spitalfields contains everything from antiques to jewelry and textiles created by design-school graduates. A market was first held in the fields near St Mary Spital hospital in the 13th century, and fruit and vegetables continued to be sold in the same area until 1991, when the market was relocated. Although the western section has been demolished, much of the Victorian structure has been preserved as an indoor space for stall-holders selling organic produce, ethnic foods and fresh bread, as well as crafts, second-hand clothes and wooden toys. The best day to catch the full range of goods is on Sunday, and every day except Saturday you can supplement your shopping energy with a stop at the Square Pie Company, a tidy, red-tiled stand serving hand-made authentic British pies in their trademark square design.

MEN'S GROOMING, HOXTON-STYLE
16 Murdock
340 Old Street

Advertising itself as 'an intimate male grooming retail space', Murdock has focused on the gap in the market for modern men's products and cosmetic services offered with the care, attention and quality of more traditional establishments, but with a spirited stylish vibe. Notice the patterned wallpaper and savvy vintage décor. Murdock offers both a selective range of independent products – such as the Santa Maria Novella range, crèmes and lathers by British makers D.R. Harris and badger-hair shaving brushes by Edwin Jagger – as well as full-service shampoo, haircut, wet shave and manicure. In addition, they stock a range of accessories, including ties by such upstanding names as Turnbull & Asser (p. 164). All in a space that is more fun-and-funky Hoxton than upper-crusty Mayfair (though they do have a concession in Liberty's).

FOOD AND FASHION ENCLAVE
17 Arnold Circus
- Rochelle Canteen, Rochelle School
- Leila's Shop, 17 Calvert Avenue
- Ally Capellino, 9 Calvert Avenue

Rochelle Canteen services the arts studios that now inhabit the old primary school, so you have to ring at the entrance to get into the former 'Boys' entrance. Opened by the team behind St John (p. 144) with a menu and décor that has quietly attracted those in gastronomic-design world, it doesn't advertise itself, but so far it hasn't needed to. For a quick and quiet coffee and snack, try neighbourhood café/deli Leila's, which had the look of a farmhouse kitchen and the feel of a friendly grocer. A few doors down, established British womenswear designer Ally Capellino keeps a surprisingly petite and sweet boutique here, near her studio, probably one of the quietest places to shop for designs rated by celebrity and fashion clients.

Three former antiques dealers have taken a spot of the dark and weary Bethnal Green Road and shined it up like a new and brightly coloured jewel. The restaurant's interiors are a riot of decorative motifs, all mixed and matched: a stuffed tiger and alligator, opulent chandeliers, bits of costume jewelry. The menu, however, reflects a lot more focus, and includes traditional French-inspired dishes from foie gras and duck breast to tiger prawns.

Before there was Jamie Oliver, there was Prue Leith, famed British chef and restaurateur, who decided to take some disadvantaged young people and give them a chance to learn the restaurant trade. The Hoxton Apprentice shows a serious commitment to making good, innovative cuisine and serving it in a place that feels sophisticated without any pretense. The menu on any given day is limited, allowing staff to focus on quality. A genuine success story for everyone, especially diners.

22 Eyre Brothers
70 Leonard Street

As one half of the team who created The Eagle (p. 138), David Eyre helped to redefine English pub food. With Eyre Brothers, David and his brother Robert have created a more sophisticated atmosphere with a cool, modern interior featuring chairs originally designed for Harry's Bar, mahogany floors and low ceilings. David Eyre has taken his Mediterranean-inspired dishes into a new realm, here focusing largely on Iberian ingredients and flavours, with a dash of Mozambique, where the Eyres grew up. Try razor clams and *jamón Ibérico* for starters and octopus with smoked paprika or hare casserole for mains.

23 Home
100–106 Leonard Street

What began as a groovy downstairs DJ bar with one room serving Mediterranean fare, has burgeoned into a fully fledged, glass-fronted hip bar and restaurant. A good first stop before hitting the bars of Hoxton Square (p. 159) and environs or a resuscitating last call (it is open until 1 am).

24 Ca4la
23 Pitfield Street

This funky little shop, formerly the atelier of Pauric Sweeney, has been taken over by one of Japan's leading manufacturers of hats. But lest you fear being one of the crowd, this is their only shop outside of Japan and their array of headwear is as weird and wonderful as the name, pronounced 'kashila' and meaning 'the head' or 'the top'.

25 White Cube
48 Hoxton Square

White Cube has become avant-garde art patron Jay Jopling's headquarters, as well as offering 2,000 square feet of open, toplit display space under 15-foot ceilings. With a list of artists that includes Damien Hirst, Tracey Emin, Nan Goldin and Lucian Freud, the gallery is a perfect insight into current – if not future – tastes in British art.

HOME FOR DESIGN
26 Her House
26 Drysdale Street

Morag Myerscough invites you to visit her at home, wander around her kitchen, sit on a sofa, and perhaps buy a design object or two. At Her House, she presents a range of contemporary design objects from a number of British makers. Artworks, furniture, ceramics and textiles are arranged much as they would be in the home – admittedly a particularly style-conscious one. A patron of emerging artists and designers, Myerscough also helps develop and produce new products under the Her House brand. In 2003 she collaborated with designer Luke Morgan to create their successful range of 'shoe plates'. The recent move to these larger premises has allowed Myerscough to hold exhibitions as well as open a café.

HIS-N-HERS FASHION
27 Start
• 59 Rivington Street (menswear)
• 42–44 Rivington Street (womenswear)

Philip Start, who founded men's label Woodhouse, and his wife Brix Smith, former guitarist with The Fall, have created a mini-fashion empire along Rivington Street with three shopfronts dedicated to their own and other selected labels. At no. 59, a dark and sleek boutique that has the feel of a gentlemen's club combined with funky Hoxton style, Start sells his own menswear line in addition to lines like Belstaff and Rykiel Homme. The women's shop is brighter and bolder, with a definite feeling of girlie glamour as well as a hip and elegant selection of daywear by high-profile and new designers, from Alexander McQueen (p. 173) to Charles Anastase and boy-wonder Alexander Wang.

ALL-NIGHTER
28 Cargo
158

GRITTY AND HIP
29 Kingsland Road
• Viet Hoa, nos 70–72
• Dreambagsjaguarshoes, nos 34–36

Kingsland Road is the place to experience an edgier emerging scene. Dreambagsjaguarshoes' vestigial sign identifying it as a former import shop belies the hipness inside created by co-owners Nick and Teresa Letchford. North of the bridge lies Viet Hoa, which many consider to be the best Vietnamese restaurant in London.

ENGLISH INTERIORS
30 Geffrye Museum
Kingsland Road

Interior design and history buffs will not be disappointed by Britain's only museum dedicated to English domestic furniture and decoration, housed in 18th-century almshouses, with a striking 1998 addition by Branson Coates. The chronological sequence of re-created period rooms begins with a 17th-century oak-panelled vignette, and progresses through the refined Georgian period, up to mid-century modern and contemporary interiors.

FLOWER-STREWN STREET
31 Columbia Road Flower Market
Columbia Road

The Columbia Road Flower Market used to be an East London tradition, but now attracts throngs of people who rise early on a Sunday to beat the crowds when the market opens at 8 am. Boasting 'the finest selection of flowers and cut plants in the country', the nursery and 'pitch' owners along the road are constantly bringing in more and increasingly exotic stock, making this one of the most picturesque open markets in Europe.

BISTRO AND BURLESQUE
32 Bistrotheque
23–27 Wadeson Street

Bistrotheque aims to answer the needs of most evening revellers: the Main Dining Room is a former industrial space painted white and retaining some of its rustic chic while offering good bistro fare; the Napoleon Room is a cosier, oak-panelled drinking den; and the Cabaret is just that, and has been credited with helping to inspire the resurgence in cabaret-style entertainment in London with the venue's trademark 'Bearlesque' show. A smaller dining room is also available for private functions.

South Bank
Southwark
Bermondsey

HOLBORN

CITY

TOWER HILL

The Tower
of London

River Thames

River Thames

Oxo
Tower
Wharf

2

Millennium
Foot
Bridge

6

Tate
Modern

5

Shakespeare's
Globe

7

4

8

Hopton St

Southwark Br

London Bridge

City Hall

Royal
National
Theatre

SOUTH BANK

SOUTHWARK

Southwark
Cathedral

14

Tooley Street

15

De
Mu

Waterloo Bridge

9

Stamford Street

Southwark Street

SOUTHWARK

Southwark   Street

LONDON
BRIDGE

19

St Thomas Street

Druid St

Drury St

Royal
Festival
Hall

Jubilee
Gardens

1

10

3

Union Street

Union Street

12

Newcomen St

Snowfields

16 **17**

Bermondsey Street

London
Eye

WATERLOO

The Cut

Blackfriars Road

Blackfriars Bridge

York Road

County Hall

Waterloo Road

11

Webber Street

Webber Street

Southwark Bridge Road

Borough High Street

BOROUGH

Long Lane

Tooley Street

Druid Street

Westminster Bridge

Houses of
Parliament

Bayliss Road

LAMBETH
NORTH

St George's
Circus

Borough Road

BOROUGH

13

Marshalsea Rd

Great Dover Street

Bermondsey
Square

18

Abbey Street

BERMON

Lambeth Palace Road

Westminster Bridge Road

Lambeth Road

St George's Road

London Road

Newington Causeway

Harper Road

Lambeth
Palace
Gardens

Lambeth
Palace

Lambeth Road

Imperial
War
Museum

Elephant
& Castle

ELEPHANT
& CASTLE

New Kent Road

Tower Bridge Road

Lambeth
Bridge

KENNINGTON

Approximate scale

1 kilometre

1/2 mile

A string of new developments, which have stop-started since the 1980s and finally culminated in the opening of Tate Modern (p. 101) in 2000, have finally galvanized the South Bank into an area greater than the sum of its parts. Until such high-profile cultural projects as the Tate and the Globe Theatre (p. 102) gave locals and visitors a reason to head south in significant numbers, efforts to rehabilitate the riverine environments, such as the South Bank Centre (p. 102), Butler's Wharf and the Design Museum, had been isolated and never really gained a critical mass. But what were once noble if disparate ventures are celebrated today as a 'string of pearls'. The London Eye (p. 100), a terrific testimony to British design and engineering, and the ovoid Greater London Authority building by Norman Foster are fitting symbols of the South Bank's arrival. The Thames River Walk provides spectacular views to the regal north shore as well as allowing a glimpse into a genuinely different side of London on the south.

Large-scale new building developments and local regeneration have in turn gradually been revivifying areas that had fallen into decay. The area immediately behind the Tate is seeing an explosion of loft developments and design studios. Local markets, such as Borough (fruit, vegetables and speciality food items; p. 106) and Bermondsey (antiques; p. 106), which have been operating for decades, if not centuries, are now attracting a more affluent clientele and international visitors. The legendary Old Vic (p. 105) received a boost when it was taken over by a charitable trust in 2000 and then raised its profile even higher when actor Kevin Spacey took over as director in 2004. The cooperative building Oxo Tower (see p. 100) symbolizes local community spirit while promoting design talent and innovative crafts. And the completion of the Millennium Bridge (p. 102) has provided further stimulus: lunching City bankers and visitors to St Paul's can stroll effortlessly across the Thames to another world.

In the last few years a number of new restaurants and bars have put Bermondsey and Borough back on the map for gastronomic destinations. Arty destinations such as Delfina (p. 106) and highly acclaimed newcomer Magdalen (p. 105) join the gallery cafés, gastropubs and cocktail bars to offer a wide range of styles and prices (though there is as yet no hotel that caters to the tastes of the chic or culture-driven traveller). As you wander down the Thames River Walk you will notice the large building works still going on, but also the improvements already made to the riverfront promenade of the Royal Festival Hall (p. 102) that makes this unequalled site once again a place for celebration.

1 London Eye
Jubilee Gardens

It was a less-publicized and non-government-funded millennium project, but it must be the most enduringly successful in terms of public enjoyment. Standing in front of the new Jubilee Gardens between the Royal Festival Hall and the County Hall and conceived by architects David Marks and Julia Barfield, the graceful giant of a Ferris wheel is a true marriage of design and engineering. Each glass-enclosed pod carries around twenty people and allows for uninterrupted views from its top height at 135 metres above the Thames. It takes thirty minutes for a full rotation of the thirty-two capsules, which means that the thrill of the ride is all in the eye.

2 Oxo Tower
Bargehouse Street

Before 1996, the places where you could have a good meal and enjoy a panoramic view of the Thames were virtually nonexistent. The Oxo Tower redevelopment, the felicitous victory of a neighbourhood coalition over hungry developers, changed all that when its top-floor restaurant and brasserie (designed by Lifshutz Davidson) opened (in association with posh department store Harvey Nichols) in the old tower building formerly belonging to the makers of bouillon cubes. The building now combines low-rent housing with retail design studios for thirty-three designers and makers on the first and second floors. The restaurant and brasserie-bar have breathtaking views and an open-air terrace. Prices tend to relate to the view rather than the food, so, given the choice, the brasserie's changing global menu is a better bet.

NEW, COOL AND SLAVIC

3 Baltic
74 Blackfriars Road

Sleek, stylish, modern and Eastern European, Baltic has turned a contemporary eye to Slavic cuisine with a cool, tasteful design more often seen in the West End than south of the river. The tall, open interior was once a workshop for a coach building, but has been stunningly remodelled. The inventive menu ranges from seasoned crayfish in vodka butter to venison with cherries, with dashes of caviar, beetroot and blinis in between. Service is as smooth as the interior decoration and low-amplitude jazz serenades the clientele venturing down from the financial district across the river. A slick bar serves a host of Polish vodkas and a spectrum of interesting, vodka-based cocktails.

THE POWER OF ART

4 Tate Modern
Bankside

The former Bankside Power Station designed by Sir Giles Gilbert Scott was opened in 1963, but by the 1990s was disused and regarded by many as an eyesore. Through the vision of Tate director Nicholas Serota and Swiss architects Herzog & de Meuron the massive building was transformed to house the collections that make up the Tate Modern, international art from 1900 to the present, including important works by Dalí, Picasso and Matisse, as well as contemporary artists. The former Turbine Hall, which runs the whole length of the vast building, makes a grand gallery entrance not unlike a cathedral space. In addition to the galleries, which feature permanent and temporary exhibitions, there is a café and art bookshop – the largest in Europe – on the ground floor. The top-floor restaurant, serving modern British cuisine, has glorious views over the Thames.

5 Tate to Tate Boat Service
Quay at Tate Modern or Tate Britain

The Tate to Tate boat service launched by Thames Clippers in 2003 follows an artistic river route from the Tate Modern (p. 101) to the original Tate Britain museum. The boat, which also makes a stop at the London Eye (p. 100), is a rather eye-catching vessel whose colourful spotty design was specially commissioned from British artist Damien Hirst. As well as transporting you from one cultural spot to the next, the boat trip allows for a fantastic cruising view of waterfront landmarks such as the Houses of Parliament, the South Bank Centre (see right) and Somerset House (p. 55).

ENGINEERING WONDER
6 Millennium Bridge
Bankside

A competition to build a pedestrian bridge spanning the Thames, the first in central London in over a century, to link the Tate Modern (p. 101) with St Paul's has resulted in what must be the most dramatic and beautiful of London's bridges. Designed by Norman Foster in collaboration with sculptor Anthony Caro and world-renowned engineering firm Arup, it is an artistic and engineering masterwork. The 325-metre-long 'blade-like' shallow bridge is an entirely new concept in suspension bridges. Walking across on a moonlit night after an evening at the Globe (see below) or dinner at the Tate, headed for the lighted, magisterial form of St Paul's, is truly an exhilarating London experience. A stroll during the day is pretty uplifting, too.

HAPPY RECREATION
7 Shakespeare's Globe
21 New Globe Walk

American actor Sam Wanamaker's dream to re-create Shakespeare's Globe Theatre was realized in 1997. With open-air wood stage and galleries, thatched roof and uncovered 'yard' – the standing area where the 'groundlings' who paid a penny for their entry would have stood while drinking beer, munching peanuts and oranges and regularly heckling the actors on stage – the Globe is a faithful reconstruction of the original Elizabethan theatre. Visitors today can stand in the yard for around five pounds. Performances, many of which are true to the 16th-century originals and highly regarded by theatre critics and public, take place in all weathers, despite the lack of a roof.

RARE AND OUT-OF-PRINT
8 Marcus Campbell Art Books
43 Holland Street

After your visit to the Tate Modern (p. 101), you might want to wander over to Marcus Campbell, conveniently located across the street. Campbell specializes in books on late-20th-century art and artists, with a particular focus on rare and out-of-print artists' books by and about such figures as Sol LeWitt, Ed Ruscha, Marcel Broodthaers, Lawrence Weiner and Gilbert and George. 'Conceptual art when it began,' Campbell says, 'and the historical stuff is what interests me.'

MAGNET FOR THE ARTS
9 South Bank Centre
- Hayward Gallery
- Royal Festival Hall
- Skylon Restaurant
- National Theatre

An extensive renovation programme of this stretch of waterfront by Rick Mather is still in progress, but so far it has already resulted in a host of improvements and is now a lively pedestrian area lined with cafés and shops. Both recently renovated, the Hayward Gallery continues to be an important venue for modern and contemporary art exhibitions and the Royal Festival Hall hosts music, dance, and literary events that are intrinsic to the diaries of most Londoners. At the top of the Royal Festival Hall, the new Skylon Restaurant (named for the original iconic building of the Festival of Britain) features a modern British menu and a raised central bar, from where you can sip cocktails and enjoy an unencumbered river view. Almost next door is the National Theatre, which runs an range of productions from Shakespeare to contemporary drama.

FOOD, GLORIOUS FOOD
10 Anchor & Hope
36 The Cut

In the current maelstrom of British gastropub dining wars, the Anchor & Hope holds its own, offering a carnival of rich, hearty eating. The dishes are well rounded with appropriate accompaniments: red cabbage, duck-fat potato cakes, lentils, prunes, figs, or a bouquet of green salad, and the interior is suitably rustic and spare. The chefs, formerly of St John (p. 144) and The Fox, another gastropub success story, have kept up an award-winning menu since opening in 2003. They don't take bookings, so get there early.

300	PETER LEHMANN, BAROSSA VALLEY, 5TH MUSE	AUSTRIA	16.00
301	BETHANY RIESLING, EDEN VALLEY, 2000	CHL.	18.75
305	DR. UNGER, GRUNER VELTLINER, 2000	CHL.	30.75
5	VIU MANENT, COLCHAGUA, CHARDONNAY, 2000	CHL.	14.75
26	MONTE VERDES, SAUVIGNON BLANC, MAIPO 2000	CHL.	18.75
24	CATENA, CHARDONNAY, VINTAGE 2000	ENG.	28.75
311	VISTA SUR, SAUV. BLANC, CENTRAL VALLEY, 2000	FR.	19.5
100	GRIBBLE BRIDGE, ORTEGA, BIDDENDEN, 2000	FR.	27.5
31	CHABLIS, DOMAINE DU COLOMBIER, 2000	FR.	17.5
35	L'EMBLEME, COLOMBARD, 2000	FR.	15.5
41	ST. VERAN, CHATEAU FUISSE, 2000	FR.	25.5
49	MUSCADET SUR LIE, DOMAINE DU VERGER, PAPIN, 2000	FR.	20.5
56	VIOGNIER GERARD BETRAND, VIN DE PAYS D'OC, 2000	FR.	30.5
302	LOUIS JADOT BOURGOGNE CHARDONNAY, 1999	GER.	27.5
58	SANCERRE, DOMAINE DU NOZAY, LOIRE 2000	GER.	
60	URZIGER WURZ, KABINET, 1996	ISRAEL	
62	URZIG ERDEN LIESEN TREPPCHEN RIESLING AUSLESE	IT.	
65	YARDEN CHARDONNAY, 2000 (KOSHER)	IT.	
72	GAVI DI GAVI "LA GIUSTINIANA"	IT.	
70	BIANCO GHIBELLINO, NEBBIOLO 1999	LUX.	
82	PINOT GRIGIO, I FUEDI DI ROMANS, 2000	NZ.	
68	RIVANER, DOMAINE CEPS D'OR, 1998	NZ.	
86	KIM CRAWFORD, PINOT GRIS 2001	NZ.	
88	SPY VALLEY, MARLBOROUGH, SAUV. BLANC, 2001	PORT.	
92	KIM CRAWFORD, MARLBOROUGH, DRY RIESLING, 2001	SA.	
95	ESPIGA BRANCA, ESTRAMADURA, 2000	SA.	
112	NICOLE'S HAT CHENIN/RIESLING, 2001	SP.	
113	WATERSIDE WHITE, GRAHAM BECK, CHARD/COLUMBARD	SP.	
110	OLD VINES, CHENIN BLANC, 2000	SP.	
119	TRES OLMOS, RUEDA SUPERIOR, VERDEJO, 2000	SF.	
121	XAREL-LO, RAVENTOS I BLANC, PENEDES, 2000	SP.	
308	TORRES FRANSOLA PENEDES, SAUV. BLANC, PARELLADA	U.	
310	MUGA BLANCO, RIOJA, VIURA MALVASIA, 2000	U.	
131	LOLONIS PRIVATE RESERVE CHARDONNAY, MENDOCINO		
135	BERINGER FUME, NAPA VALLEY, SAUV. BLANC, 1999		
307	GLEN ELLEN WINERY, CALIFORNIA, CHARDONNAY, 1998		
309	BEAULIEU VINEYARD, COASTAL CHARD, CALIFORNIA, 1999		

11 Old Vic Theatre
The Cut

One of the oldest theatres in London and the only surviving venue dating from the Regency period (founded 1818), the Old Vic has a worldwide reputation as 'the actors' theatre'. Laurence Olivier, John Gielgud, Alec Guiness, Ralph Richardson, Peter O'Toole, Judi Dench and Maggie Smith have all trod the boards here, but the future was in jeopardy when the theatre came up for sale. Fortunately a charitable trust took over in 2000, and popular interest grew when Kevin Spacey took over as director in 2004. His first production, the dark comedy *Cloaca*, by Dutch writer Maria Goos got mixed reviews, but such teething problems haven't dimmed the bright future predicted for the old favourite under Spacey's guidance.

HISTORIC PLEASURE
12 The George Inn
77 Borough High Street

On a cobbled courtyard off Borough High Street is London's only surviving galleried coaching inn, a rare example of a medieval pub in the city. Destroyed by fire and rebuilt in 1676, it has escaped demolition many times and is now protected by the National Trust. Its distinctive white-washed but yellowed walls, oak beams, wood panelling and lattice windows evoke another era beyond the modern-day traffic outside. Dickens is said to have been a regular in one of the series of room-sized bars that make up the ground floor. The former bedchambers upstairs have long since been converted to dining and public rooms, but have lost none of their gloriously aged character in the transition.

CITY OF WINE
13 Vinopolis
1 Bank End

'Uncork your mind; indulge your senses' is the motto of this modern temple to the grape along the Millennium Mile on the South Bank of the Thames. A wine museum that features an interactive virtual tour through all the wine-growing regions of the world, it contains enough history and information to make you drunk on facts. Luckily there is also the revered product itself, available at tasting tables along the way and sold in the adjacent wine store. Even if you're just stopping by, there's a vast selection to be had by the glass or bottle in the Wine Wharf bar, as well as in the Michelin-rated Cantina Vinopolis.

GOTHIC ORIGINAL
14 Southwark Cathedral
Montague Close

The earliest Gothic church in London was built as St Mary Overie in 1220 and became the parish church of St Saviour, Southwark, in 1539. It suffered fires and periods of neglect until it was bought from James I in 1614 by the parishioners, who have looked after it ever since. Happily, it was not damaged during the Civil War, and the current tower with four pinnacles was finished in 1689. Among the many wonderful tributes, monuments and gifts inside is a 13th-century carved oak effigy of a knight and another of John Gower, who was a friend to Chaucer and himself a poet (Chaucer's pilgrims in the *Canterbury Tales* set off from a spot near here). Inside the southwest entrance the Gothic arcading is still visible, which was rebuilt after a fire in 1206. At one end of the north aisle are twelve ceiling bosses taken from the 15th-century wooden roof that collapsed in 1830. They depict vices such as malice, gluttony and falsehood, as well as heraldic sunflowers and roses. Piers, chancel and other elements from the 13th century have survived, along with many wonderful later pieces, such as the carved monument to Alderman Humble and his wives, dressed in their 17th-century best. The monument to Shakespeare is modern, but there is a funeral paving stone belonging to the Bard's brother Edmund (d. 1607).

STAR-STUDDED CHEFS
15 Magdalen Restaurant
152 Tooley Street

This is one of a few relatively new restaurants in London – see also Wild Honey (p. 44), Arbutus (p. 137) and Tom's Kitchen (p. 31) – that had critics revelling in near-embarrassing praise of its food. But with such a pedigree – head chef James Faulks worked with Heston Blumenthal at the Fat Duck (p. 182) before moving to the Anchor & Hope (p. 102), pastry chef Emma Faulks was previously at the Mandarin Oriental, and David Abbott came from Le Manoir aux Quat'Saisons – expectations were going to be high. Even more amazing than that, they have managed to exceed them with a British-based menu that offers a full range of well-sourced meat and game, as well as fish, crab and vegetarian plates, prepared with exceeding skill. Try hard to leave room for dessert.

16 Delfina

50 Bermondsey Street

Located on a characterful street, Delfina started out as a warehouse that had been converted into studio space for artists by patron Delfina Entrecanales. The café for resident artists soon became a popular lunchtime spot, and today it helps to support the studio programme and provides public exhibition space. Its white-walled surroundings are a fitting backdrop to the changing collection of artworks, and even the labels on the wine bottles are works of art, produced by Turner Prize-nominee Tacita Dean. Maria Eilia is the artist in the kitchen, producing modern Mediterranean dishes such as seared tuna and chorizo risotto, in a menu that changes fortnightly.

DESTINATION SOUTH
17 Bermondsey Street

- Fashion and Textile Museum, no. 83
- The Garrison, no. 99
- Village East, nos 171–173
- Cockfighter of Bermondsey, no. 96
- Holly & Lil, no. 103

Another area of London that is enjoying the march of property buyers and regeneration, Bermondsey Street is now bursting with new independent shops and restaurants. Its fortunes began to revive with the opening of Delfina (see above) and the Fashion and Textile Museum, created by fashion designer Zandra Rhodes with the help of Mexican architect Ricardo Legorreta, which is a bold pink-and-orange paean to the work of local and international designers. The Garrison is a pub that, rather than being stripped of all its character, has been dressed up with a pretty antique chic décor in a warm, welcoming rustic shell and serves good modern English food. The same team behind The Garrison recently converted larger premises farther along Bermondsey Street into Village East, a bright, multi-level contemporary eating and drinking space with comfy seating in the bar area that fills up with newly southward-bound clientele in the evening. The funky streetwear designers at Cockfighter of Bermondsey, Kate Linden and Damian Wilson, give the area its own cultwear fashion cred with their range of own-label T-shirts and accessories. Opposite at Holly & Lil, you can find that truly unique gift for your pet or pet-loving friend back home: hand-made leather and diamante-studded dog collars and leashes. So stylish, they're not to be sniffed at.

LEGENDARY ANTIQUES
18 Bermondsey Market

Bermondsey Square

This pre-dawn, Friday-only market held in a quiet square has legendary status among Londoners. The enchantment has to do with its early opening hours, a consequence, it is generally believed, of the fact that objects sold before sunrise are not subject to laws regarding the handling of stolen goods. The reality is that this is London's most vibrant antiques market, a feeding ground mostly for dealers and knowledgable early risers – prices do so after 9 am. Jewelry and silver are the mainstays of the market, but paintings, china, rugs and a host of bric-à-brac are all to be had for the right, often negotiable, sum.

SERIOUS FOODIES ONLY
19 Borough Market

- Roast, The Floral Hall, Stoney Street
- Wright Brothers, 11 Stoney Street

One of the largest food markets in the world, Borough Market is still unknown to many Londoners who keep their shopping north of the river. This makes no difference to the thriving pace of buying, selling, strolling, eating and drinking, which has been going on here since the Romans built the original London Bridge. As well as a popular fruit and vegetable market, Borough is also a source of fine foods for many London chefs. The recent influx of more affluent residents has also brought a new wave of cafés and restaurants to the area. One of the first to attract attention was Roast, which opened in 2005 on the top floor of the Floral Hall and offers modern British food with ingredients sourced from the UK. Wright Brothers began by supplying French oysters to fine London restaurants and hotels, later opening this bar to serve their acclaimed fresh seafood and quality beer and ale.

Style Traveller

sleep • eat • drink
shop • retreat

sleep

London's best hotels are famed for their discreet service and attention to detail. Although it was not until relatively recently that London responded to the global trend for stylish, more individualistic accommodation, there is now an incomparable array of establishments, ranging from the ultra-modern to the ingeniously or ironically traditional. Here is a selection of the best hard-to-find hideaways: small mid-modern meccas, accessibly grand boltholes and over-the-top tributes to minimalism, their distinct character reflecting the charisma and vision of their founders.

84	**The Hoxton Urban Lodge**
6	81 Great Eastern Street
	Rooms from £29

As Hoxton grew from groovy arty area to burgeoning bourgeois enclave, it was only a matter of time before it got its own trendy hotel. However, this is really hotelling Hoxton-style, where the usual exposed brick and vintage touches combine with laudable amenities and top-notch services to make for rooms with a comfortably bohemian view. Offering something like no-frills luxury (they call it a 'luxury budget hotel'), the Hoxton strives to do the basics very well so that guests are not bombarded with (and charged for) unnecessary extras. The result is that guests are well cared for in slightly funky and unusual style. With 205 rooms over six floors, this isn't exactly boutique-hotel territory, but neither is it an anonymous corporate giant. Rooms include Frette linens and down duvets, sleek tiled bathrooms with power showers, flat-screen televisions, WiFi and 'lite' breakfasts provided by every Londoner's favourite fast sandwich- and croissant-fix, Pret à Manger, whose founder is the brains behind the Hoxton. All rooms have a desk and sofa, so there are no business-traveller broom-closet specials. And at the prices available for a room at the Hoxton, who needs them? The artful touches are much more interesting than one would expect for anything with 'budget' in the description.

The Hoxton Grille on the ground floor is a 'modern brasserie' restaurant and lounge bar that serves breakfast lunch, dinner and rather lovely cocktails, which is a good thing since the rooms do not have minibars. The gym and swimming pool are not on-site and not included in your room charge, rather they are located at the nearby Market Sports club and cost only an extra £5 per visit. Close to all of the happenings on the Hoxton scene, any added frills you might need are just a short walk away.

Benedict Radcliffe
Modern Japanese Classic

70
The Zetter
29 St John's Square, 86–88 Clerkenwell Road
Rooms from £150

Period architecture with contemporary design flair; all mod cons and an environmental conscience, hip location and reasonable rates: The Zetter is a host of lively contrasts. Michael Benyan and Mark Sainsbury, the duo behind The Zetter, have had a string of restaurant successes behind them: the Quality Chop House (p. 78) and, with Sam and Sam Clark, Moro (p. 79), among them. With The Zetter they combined a stylish bar and restaurant on the ground floor with rooms located around an atrium above, in their words 'a modern-day urban inn', where people could 'meet, eat or sleep'. Beyond that they managed successfully to integrate the historic architecture of a Victorian warehouse building with minimal but striking elements of new design. With fifty-nine rooms on five floors, The Zetter maintains a high level of quality and comfort on a relatively small scale. At the top of the building, seven rooftop studios have been added on with floor-to-ceiling windows and French doors leading to rooftop patio spaces.

Design touches such as art pieces, textiles and wall panels add glamour to the large-proportioned spaces, while home comforts include hot-water bottles and books for borrowing. The Zetter also has eco cred, and sustainable materials were used in the design: the bathroom basins are made from recycled plastic; the atrium provides natural ventilation; and the hotel has its own well, which in addition to providing water for air conditioning, is also the source for the still and sparkling drinking water on offer. Situated near the confluence of the financial centre of the City, the cultural hub of Bloomsbury and the bohemian base of Clerkenwell, The Zetter provides guests with a starting point for a range of London experiences. Crafts by local makers are available at the Penneybank studios just behind the hotel in St John's Square, and some of the city's best new British cuisine is to be had at St John, just a few minutes' walk away (p. 144).

LITERARY LAIR

42 **Hazlitt's**

38 6 Frith Street
Rooms from £240

'In art, in taste, in life, in speech, you decide from feeling, and not from reason.' So wrote the great essayist, critic and Napoleon biographer William Hazlitt in 1822. With such inspiration in mind, Douglas Bain and Peter McKay (see also The Rookery; p. 120) set out to create a home away from home in a set of three of Soho's most characterful houses, built in 1718 and where Hazlitt died, purportedly of drinking too much tea, on 18 September 1830 in what was then a boarding house. Set on a bustling street and surrounded by creative agencies, restaurants and bars, Hazlitt's is a world away from 21st-century global London, a discreet and intimate hideaway from the modern world. Guests who desire a long-lost quintessentially English experience will experience the words that Hazlitt requested for his gravestone: 'grateful and contented'.

But don't let the twenty-three rooms' mahogany four-poster beds and Victorian claw-foot tubs (some original to the house), the rich, bold colours of the walls and fabrics (the hotel was completely remodelled in 2001), the small sitting rooms and wonky floors and the absence of elevators fool you, this is the haunt of the media, antiques collectors and dignitaries who sense that there is something very special about Hazlitt's and far removed from corporate modern. The staff might be stylish and amenities contemporary, but the contrast wouldn't have bothered Hazlitt, who observed, 'We are not hypocrites in our sleep.'

28 **Cadogan London**
19 75 Sloane Street
Rooms from £290

Completed in 1888, this hotel is now forever associated with its two most prominent patrons, Lillie Langtry and Oscar Wilde. Langtry, mistress of Edward VII, lived at 21 Pont Street, which became amalgamated with the hotel. Wilde, who was an admirer of the famous actress and stayed at the Cadogan partly in order to be close to her, was arrested here on charges of having committed offences against young men, and escorted from room 118, now the Oscar Wilde Room. The hotel had become a bit rough around the edges when Grace Leo-Andrieu took over management and oversaw the redecoration of the first two floors in 2003. Now the ground-floor public rooms are shined up in period splendour, with swag draperies, polished woodwork and grand proportions, and even the conference room has a touch of period elegance about it.

The crowning achievements, however, are the rooms named for the Cadogan's most famous residents. The Lillie Langtry is all fluff and flowers, a boudoir bedecked in rose wallpaper, pink lace, satin and feather boas. Added to the feminine finery is the prime position of the room overlooking Sloane Square. The Oscar Wilde is somewhat more masculine but no less indulgent, with blue-grey velvet and silvery taffeta. A corner room, it features a bay of three windows that emphasize the tall ceiling height. Other rooms are more restrained but carry the theme of fine furnishing and luxurious fabrics throughout. Rooms on the upper floors have yet to be refurbished, but retain an old-fashioned charm that has been brightened with modern touches. All residents are allowed access to the lovely Cadogan Gardens and tennis courts across from the hotel, which are only open to residents. Shopping and dining in Pont Street, Sloane Square and most of Knightsbridge is within walking distance. Top off your visit with a meal at Tom Aikens (p. 145) for luxury of a more contemporary kind.

It is hard to say what delights most about this hidden gem. There is the tricky access off a tree-shaded, pedestrianized alley near bustling Smithfield Market, before one steps across the threshold of what seems like someone's private house. Once inside, there are the thirty-three eccentrically appointed bedrooms, each named after a local character who once lived nearby, thus imbuing the four Georgian houses that make up this quintessentially London townhouse hotel not only with period charm, but with real personality. Smithfield was once known for lawlessness – Charles Dickens' Fagin is said to have haunted its streets – being outside the City's jurisdiction; areas such as these were known as 'rookeries'. Though Smithfield is now full of smartly dressed City workers and restaurant patrons, the edgy atmosphere has not completely disappeared, which makes for a rather irresistible mix of old-world intrigue and modern sophistication.

As you might expect, The Rookery is a labour of love, created by Douglas Bain and Peter McKay (see also Hazlitt's; p. 116), who have artfully combined the old and new in a romantically quirky yet detail-conscious atmosphere. All of the modern amenities are on tap, while a careful refurbishment of the original furnishings and fittings (wardrobes, secretaires, great carved four-poster beds or Gothic-style bedsteads, period oak panelling, even the Victorian commodes) that draws on Bain and McKay's extensive antiques knowledge has taken place with the idea that 'history is always more appealing when it has been cleaned up a bit'. Specialist craftsmen were hired to restore the period plumbing fixtures and adapt them to modern pipework.

The hotel's *pièce de résistance* is the incomparable 'Rook's Nest', a top-level suite with the same carefully honed period feel, enhanced by a restored Edwardian bathing machine, but with a hidden extra: the ceiling opens to reveal a rooftop sitting room accessed by a small stair where guests can enjoy their own private panorama of London. Downstairs, life is less heady, but no less luxurious.

42 **The Haymarket Hotel**

28 1 Suffolk Place
Rooms from £245

The American Express office and four townhouses that occupied this Regency building designed by John Nash have been swept away in a seemingly effortless transformation to a modern English country-style hotel under the knowing direction of Kit and Tim Kemp. The Kemps have already worked their design magic with the Charlotte Street, Knightsbridge and Pelham hotels, and here they bring their very distinctive mix of traditional and contemporary British luxury living to the heart of The Haymarket. This is a sanctuary of visual delights from the busy nearby streets, where tourist kitsch jostles with theatre bills against a constant stream of traffic.

The ground-floor spaces are well mannered and grandly appointed, with separate areas for meeting, reading and relaxing. Salon lighting and intimate seating in the conservatory and library contrast with great swathes of tropical wallcovering and ornate mirrors recalling elegant colonial largesse in the function room. In the basement, an 18-metre pool and bar area caters to the need for fitness and/or indulgence. Above stairs, there are fifty rooms and one separate townhouse, each decorated with an individually orchestrated selection of colours, prints and patterns from the Kit Kemp palette of sumptuous ambience. You won't find this degree of decorative detail anywhere else. All the rooms, from the smallest bedrooms to the largest suites have minibars, wireless access and flat-screen televisions. The one- and two-bedroom suites have a separate drawing room, hallway and one or two bathrooms, and each guestroom or suite is decked out in an array of beautiful fabrics and plush upholstery guided by a well-honed knack for comfort in bedding and bathroom amenities, including exclusive products by UK fragrance designer Miller Harris (p. 20) – almost an excuse to book a room in itself. The Brumus bar and restaurant on the ground floor is part of the hotel and is open every day.

28 Eleven Cadogan Gardens

18 11 Cadogan Gardens
Rooms from £240

A stone's throw from Sloane Square, marked only by a single sign 'No 11', Eleven Cadogan Gardens is a genuine late Victorian testament to what makes the English hotel unique: understatement, discretion, an apparently undesigned interior that works wonderfully, and a just a hint of the aristocratic. It's not hard to understand why it is reportedly design guru Philippe Starck's favourite London hotel. Though one must resist the urge to use superlatives (particularly inappropriate in this context), there is an authenticity, warmth and ease that makes a stay at Eleven Cadogan Gardens an experience you would have only here, in the heart of Chelsea, which means that the high volume of loyal repeat guests can make getting a room tricky at times.

The establishment began life in the late 19th century, when Lord Chelsea built four mansions on his cricket ground near Buckingham Palace, which soon become London's first private townhouse hotel. Today, there remain sixty rooms (ask for one of the ones at the back, which overlook beautifully manicured gardens), rich wood-panelled walls, oil paintings, an oak staircase and countless antiques, along with two Garden Suites, one that offers a private entrance and the other featuring a large drawing room that overlooks the garden.

There is no reception desk, but a butler greets visitors at the door, signifying the level of service to follow. Guests sign a well-worn ledger before being escorted to their premises. Tucked discreetly away in the building are modern amenities, such as a gym and beauty treatment room; reluctant concessions, no doubt, to contemporary travellers. To round out the picture, guests are offered afternoon tea in the dining room, along with fresh cakes, sherry and canapes – what else?

48 The Fox Club London

20 46 Clarges Street
Rooms from £110

The early 18th-century townhouse was built in an area dominated by large mansions commissioned by members of the landed aristocracy, such as Lord Berkeley and the Earl of Clarendon. Named for the legendary orator and charismatic Whig statesman Charles James Fox (1749–1806), the house actually belonged to his mistress and later wife, Elizabeth Armistead, who worked in a common brothel before being taken in by the Viscount Bolingbroke (married and then divorced from Lady Diana Spencer), later becoming an actress and courtesan to a succession of wealthy swooning gentlemen. Mrs Armistead bought the property on Clarges Street some time in the 1780s. In the recent past the house has served variously as a hotel or rooming house, but has fortunately preserved most of its alluring decorative details and Georgian character and remains an intimate, welcoming place that offers the comfort and charm of an historic private home away from home. Set on a quiet, unassuming street, not wholly immune to the air of discreet assignations, it does little to announce itself and much to draw a loyal following.

The current owners took over in 2005 and created this combination private club and boutique hotel. Though there is a membership available, anyone can book one of the nine rooms, all named after various lovers of Mrs Armistead, such as Fox himself, George IV, Lord Dorset and Lord 'Bully' Bolingbroke. All rooms have private bathrooms recently refurbished in slick marble and chrome and supplied with Molton Brown products. However, the bedrooms retain a reassuringly quaint flavour with mixtures of fabrics, swagged headboards and eclectic touches. There is no room service, but a continental breakfast is served in the Georgian-period lounge with its quaint pewter bar and a chef is on duty during the day, Monday through Friday; special dinners can be arranged in advance.

[14]

HOME FROM HOME
The Main House
[29]
6 Colville Road
Rooms from £100

Caroline Main isn't exactly rushing around trying to fill her four-room/three-suite hotel located around the corner from what is probably Notting Hill's most fashionable 200-metre stretch. In fact, she has never advertised at all during the three years that she has been operating The Main House, but then she hasn't needed to. Word of mouth is enough to keep this spacious Victorian house, with unmarked entrance, relatively full for most of the year. But it's hard to keep a secret, especially the one about very reasonably priced, roomy, stylish accommodation in London with personalized service that makes you wonder why you ever settled for less. 'Simple and professional' is Main's mantra, and it applies to everything from the furnishings (though you could also add a certain flair for design here) to the taxi service she offers to collect you and your luggage from the airport, for which you pay only the fee to the taxi company.

She is equally strict about the running of The Main House, whose rooms have been stripped of fussy decoration but retain period details and generous proportions. These are not highly kitted-out boxes, but airy spaces with large windows, polished wood floors, a few choice antique furnishings and rugs and lots of fresh white linens. The first- and second-floor rooms, true to their Victorian design, are the grandest in terms of space and include separate sitting and bath areas, one suite per floor. The top floor is given over to two rooms and a smaller shower room, usually let as a suite for families or people travelling together. Main herself is often on call, along with manager Beatta, to bring tea, biscuits, wine, give local advice and arrange taxis. Guests are free to entertain their own visitors, and a separate doorbell even allows them to answer the door themselves – just like home. This and the lack of signage means that it feels more like a house, says Main. So there, the secret is out.

eat

In the past, few visitors would have seen London as a culinary destination, but this preconception has changed radically over the last ten years or so. A variety of ethnic restaurants has also been an aspect of the city's cosmopolitanism, but today offers more choice than ever before – everything from European cuisine at the very highest level to exotic fare updated with Western touches. Where London has seen the most notable – and, for the world gourmand, most intriguing – development is in the celebration of its own culinary traditions. Where once the visitor faced 'pub grub', today there is a profusion of 'gastropubs', bars serving well-prepared dishes using fresh local ingredients, and a new British cuisine tailored to today's more international and demanding palates.

42 **Umu**

12 14–16 Bruton Place

There seems to be something of an Oriental invasion happening in the London restaurant scene with Roka (p. 62), Yauatcha (p. 141) and Hakkasan (opposite) drawing crowds of upscale diners. Now Umu, an ultra-modern, chic, sophisticated temple of cuisine has arrived with an entrance on Bruton Place so discreet that it's in danger of being overlooked. But it isn't just gimmicky restaurateuring that should bring you to Umu. The décor is wonderful and you do have to press your hand to an electronic glass panel to slide open the unmarked front door, but these details are supremely matched by the food, which is traditional Kyoto-style and served either in a set menu or as a range of *kaiseiki* options, which are small, beautifully crafted portions. The proprietors are keen to stay true to their roots, even importing water from Japan for some of the cooking. Fish is sourced from all over the world, and a sushi bar lets you get a close look at each species. But such artistic and culinary opulence comes at a price, so be prepared for triple digits.

42 St Alban

6 4–12 Regent Street

The sensuous round corner entrance, with its etched glass panels decorated with large-scale line drawings, keeps the public from gaping a view into this hive of modern style and cooking, and helps set the tone of a quiet retreat from the masses. But this new restaurant, created by Chris Corbin and Jeremy King (who also brought us The Wolseley; p. 136), is more about good food in inspired surroundings than exclusivity. There are works of art on the walls and some rather crashing (though invigorating) colour combinations, but the menu really wins the day. A varied selection of traditional and more inventive dishes includes pizza (at lunchtime), as well as squid in ink with chilli, crab, slow-roasted pig, pasta and risotto. Wines are well chosen, as expected, and the service is well-nigh impeccable.

58 Hakkasan

15 8 Hanway Place

As you make your way from the teeming throngs of Tottenham Court Road and Oxford Street down a rather unsavoury alleyway, nothing can prepare you for this exquisite bar and restaurant, which combines stylish modern-exotic design with a delicate Singaporean-tinged cuisine. Through the doors you step out of a gritty urban backstreet down into a seductively lit, slate-lined stair and into a sensuous aquamarine environment masterfully created by French designer Christian Liaigre. London's fashionable set prefer to queue for the evening scene, but the best time to go is at lunch, when a modern dim sum menu, prepared by head chef Tong Chee Hwee (formerly of the Summer Pavilion at Singapore's Ritz Carlton), is available against purple-illuminated glass, fretted-wood partitions and dark wood – continents away from London and worlds away from the mass retail frenzy above. You needn't stop at dim sum, as a more complete, contemporary Chinese menu for lunch and dinner is available, as are Asian-tinted cocktails conceived by one of London's master mixers.

Rules

35 Maiden Lane

Claiming to be London's oldest restaurant, Rules has been
going continuously since Thomas Rule first opened it in
1798, when it was known for its 'porter, pies and oysters'.
Over the centuries, royalty and celebrity have filled its
dining room: it was known as the haunt of Edward VII
when Prince of Wales and his mistress, the actress Lillie
Langtry, who made such a habit of visiting that a private
door was added so they could avoid the prying eyes of the
public, and Charles Dickens, Graham Greene and H. G.
Wells were also frequent diners. It is still devoted to
distinctly British meat and game – rabbit, deer, grouse
and the prized Belted Galloway cattle – which comes
directly from the restaurant's own estates in Lartington in
the High Pennines to ensure the highest standards.
A recently restored and beautifully atmospheric dining
room, preserved by the last of only three owning families
over the decades, provides handsomely for the 'rakes,
dandies and superior intelligences who comprise its
clientele'. Living London culture and history are alive and
well in Covent Garden.

QUIET AND CLUBBY

42 **Adam Street**

50 9 Adam Street

Like the most intriguing city addresses, you wouldn't know it was there unless you were looking for it. A plaque announces a private members' club just off the Strand, and the bell suggests that the uninvited are not to wander in. Fortunately you don't have to be a member to book a table in the restaurant for lunch, though descending the red-carpeted staircase does deliver the zing of exclusivity. As you step into the subterranean space, you might remember that the dual barrel vaults in which the restaurant and bar are now situated were the foundations of the Adelphi, a development of artists' residences conceived and partly built by master architects Robert and James Adam from 1768 to 1792. Today the space has been modernized, peopled with nearby publishers and features a bar area, with contemporary club chairs and purple velvet stools, while the restaurant is a formal, intimate dining space with classic British dishes (including a revisited macaroni and cheese). A destination after morning gallery visits on Trafalgar Square.

TOWNHOUSE DINING

42 **Lindsay House**

35 21 Romilly Street

Irish chef Richard Corrigan was awarded a Michelin star for this restaurant, which occupies a 1740 London townhouse in the heart of Soho. Though set in an atmosphere of cheap Italian cafés, pubs and sex shops, the genteel and serene atmosphere of Lindsay House – which begins as soon as you ring the entrance doorbell – sits in stark contrast to the revelling hoi polloi outside. Two Georgian dining rooms, with preserved period details, high ceilings and minimally added decoration, have an elegantly at-home feel about them, which, despite the high ratio of staff to diners, makes for a warm, intimate and ultimately romantic experience. The menu encompasses a range of lightly fused cuisines from gazpacho of English crayfish to guinea fowl in Madeira, and the wine list is varied and well suited to the exquisitely prepared dishes.

ARCHETYPAL CARVERY
42 The Grill Room
2 Dorchester Hotel, 53 Park Lane

It's really a shame to visit London without splashing out for a proper carvery in one of the classic grand hotel restaurants. Merely uttering 'The Dorchester' carries a ring of refinement that becomes evident beneath the great Grill Room's gold-leaf-lined coffered ceiling and among the leather armchairs, velvet curtains and Flemish tapestries, all of which are from the 1931 room, when it was known as the Spanish Grill and featured a dedicated sherry bar. Today, the menu celebrates high British cuisine. Head chef Aiden Byrne, who came to The Grill Room in 2006 after a period at Tom Aikens (p. 145), has embraced the traditional fare with a passion: main courses include roast Aberdeenshire beef with Yorkshire pudding, rack of pork with glazed apple and Atlantic cod with red-pepper crust and pickled anchovies. Byrne's signature dishes are variations on the traditional – cottage pie, made with veal fillet and served in four different ways, and a modern take on bread & butter pudding. Having had only eight chefs in the last seventy-five years, The Grill Room stands as a timeless and unwavering London institution.

OH, VIENNA
42 The Wolseley
26 160 Piccadilly

The Wolseley opened in 2003 to almost instant acclaim and doesn't seem to be losing any popularity. Founders of star-attractors Le Caprice and the Ivy (along with St Alban; p. 133) – Jeremy King and Christopher Corbin – took over this former car showroom to open a grand Old World café, with a design by David Collins (see Blue Bar; p. 151). The great ceiling space, brass-lined bar, reading lamps, treat-filled pastry counter, starched white tablecloths and formally trained but friendly staff make The Wolseley popular with both famous and casual diners. The menu is old-fashioned as well, offering steaks cooked to perfection whichever way you ask for them, and delicately cut chips (if chips can ever be delicate) presented in a jolly paper-wrapped parcel for lunch. Chef Chris Galvin, who once presided over the Michelin-starred Orrery, has since moved on, but the omelettes, bratwurst, oysters and caviar still conspire to make customers feel like a Habsburg on holiday. Alas, you have a much better chance of getting in for lunch or the Viennoisserie-style breakfast than for dinner, which is sometimes booked weeks in advance.

42 **Arbutus**
41 63–64 Frith Street

Anthony Demetre and Will Smith opened this bastion of fine dining in Soho in 2006 and won immediate praise, not surprising since Demetre had previously been awarded a Michelin star for his menu at Putney Bridge. However, they appear to go from strength to strength as the menu of hearty British cooking lightened with new twists and influences keeps Arbutus humming at lunch and dinner. The menu changes weekly according to seasonal produce, but enticing examples include a ravioli of Limousin veal, squid and mackerel burger and English kale and potato soup. The wine list offers a host of appealing options, especially as all of the wines are available by the third-of-a-bottle (250-ml) carafe, and this includes around twenty-five reds and another twenty-five whites, rosés and dessert wines. The pair have managed to add a second restaurant that is proving just as popular with London's gastro-intelligentsia (see Wild Honey; p. 44).

NEIGHBOURHOOD JOINT

The Cow

15 89 Westbourne Park Road

The Cow, at the periphery of Notting Hill, was a pleasant old-fashioned pub even before it became known for its new menu and speciality, fresh seafood. Owned by Tom Conran, son of restaurateur and design guru Terence, today it is a little pub with a large following and a jolly place to meet for a drink and a plate of oysters, a little slice of Notting Hill life and a favourite of locals despite the occasional visit from a celebrity (Elvis Costello, Uma Thurman, Kylie Minogue and Hugh Grant have stopped by). If a heartier meal is in your sights, you can have a proper repast in the intimate upstairs dining room, which focuses on modern British (you are advised to book ahead). In nice weather, sitting outside on the quiet road in view of the nearby Westbourne (p. 20), you might feel a little spoiled for choice.

THE ORIGINAL GASTROPUB

The Eagle

24 159 Farringdon Road

Hailed as the first 'gastropub' in London, The Eagle began in 1991 what many modernized London pubs are now trying to do with widely varying degrees of success. As owner Michael Belben, who started The Eagle with David Eyre (see Eyre Brothers; p. 93), its first chef, says: 'We weren't the first pub to serve good food, but we were probably the first to serve extremely good food in casual surroundings.' What they did not want to do was 'exclude traditional drinkers', nor did they want to include a lot of 'unnecessary trimmings'. So you won't find table linens or complicated selections of courses, or even a tab (you pay when you order), but you will find a place that's welcoming for a long drink or a very good dinner, as enjoyed by the nearby journalists and creatives. Wood details and an eclectic mix of well-worn leather sofas, old bar stools and unmatched dining chairs contribute to the casual atmosphere. The daily-changing menu is hearty and leans toward the Mediterranean, though current chef Tom Norrington-Davis says this is because they serve what they think is good, not because they're adhering to style.

42 **Cinnamon Club**

53 30–32 Great Smith Street

All-white tablecloths and high-backed chairs arranged against magnificent soaring white walls in what used to be the 1897 Westminster Library, the Cinnamon Club is the modern, upscale face of Indian food as envisioned by owner Iqbal Wahhab. Original bookshelves, wood screens and parquet flooring have been retained, while Indian marble and stone have been incorporated into a clean-lined fusion of colonial convergence. Under chef Vivek Singh, with the help of Michelin-starred French chef Eric Chavot, contemporary Indian cuisine reaches new heights of sophistication and refinement, served to a public ranging from Westminster politicians to jet-setters. Traditional techniques are applied to unconventional ingredients and vice versa, producing acclaimed dishes such as sweet potato cake with crispy okra and spiced yoghurt, duck breast with sesame tamarind sauce, and spinach dumplings with chickpea cake, all suggesting that this is a place with staying power. The downstairs late-night members' bar and lounge offers Indian-tinged cocktails and dance music to ensure your evening ends on a cool note.

Sketch

8 9 Conduit Street

Among the most ambitious and chicest venues to open in the last decade, Sketch (so-called because it is constantly evolving) marks the apotheosis of high design, high style and high gastronomy. A long-term labour of love and passion by Mourad Mazouz and set in a Georgian mansion most recently occupied by Christian Dior, Sketch displays a dazzling diversity of design that extends to a parlour, art gallery, two bars, two restaurants and a lecture theatre. No surface, from the Swarovski-bejeweled bathrooms to the in-situ artworks, has been left unconsidered; no culinary delight thought too extravagant (Parisian masterchef Pierre Gagnaire has created all the food, from the pastries in the parlour to the Library restaurant's haute cuisine – probably the most expensive in Britain); and no possibility for design overlooked, from the carts in the Gallery restaurant by Marc Newson and the East Bar's toilet pods to the custom furniture pieces by Noé Duchaufour Lawrance. A total work of art for all the senses, Sketch sets new standards in the urban epicurean experience.

DIM SUM AND THEN SOME

42 **Yauatcha**

30 15 Broadwick Street

With a white-themed interior conceived by Christian Liaigre, a menu overseen by Cheong Wah Soon (both of whom had a similarly successful input at Hakkasan; p. 133), uniforms designed by Tom Yip, costume designer for *Crouching Tiger, Hidden Dragon,* and staff that seem to have invented the terms 'simple' and 'elegant', Yauatcha is a den of taste in all of its conceivable meanings. Alan Yau, restaurateur behind the popular Wagamama noodle bars and Hakkasan has brought a touch of Cantonese class to Soho. Removed in more ways than one from the kitsch clamour of nearby Chinatown, Yauatcha offers the highest quality dim sum, as well as tea and colourful cocktails, all day long in the lower-ground-floor restaurant. There is also the bright, retro-futuristic bubble of the ground-floor tea room, which is highly visible from outside, drawing diners as well as curious passers-by. Here, tea and cakes are served or, if you like, beautifully packaged to take home or present as stylish gourmet gifts. This is dim sum dining, yes, but with a thoroughly London, style-conscious presentation that puts it in a category of its own.

42 **Scott's**

4 20 Mount Street

The forces behind the Ivy and J. Sheekey (p. 50) have been at it again, this time reclaiming a mid-19th-century fish restaurant and turning it into a near theatrical experience. The restaurant reflects its well-heeled neighbourhood surroundings and has proved harder to get into than many an élite club, but once you're there you might as well indulge in the atmosphere of finery that pervades everything from the scalloped mosaic flooring to the well-folded napkins. The menu centres on seafood, and what better way to celebrate fish-eating than with a luxury ocean-liner inspired bar complete with crustaceans gloriously on display, glittering chandeliers and an army of staff ready with plates for bones and shells or another glass of perfectly matched Riesling. Aside from the various plates of John Dory, prawns, crab and skate, expect to find five kinds of oysters and three different caviars, as well as meat and game dishes.

42 **Red Fort**
37 77 Dean Street

A shining example of high-style Indian cuisine ('the mother of Indian restaurants' it was dubbed by one publication in the know) even before its relaunch in 2000 after being destroyed by a fire, what was once a classic has reinvented itself with an even greater commitment to contemporary cuisine, style and service. The recent incarnation pays homage to the original Red Fort, built in Delhi by Shah Jahan, who also built the Taj Mahal, by incorporating the same materials but updated to contemporary demands in a lush and sultry setting. The menu is produced by chef Mohammed Rais, who comes from a 300-year line of court chefs and who has mastered the art of *dum pukht*, a form of steam cooking, which imbues regional *biryanis* with an added edge. A wide selection of refined dishes includes *dum ka* lobster, which has been steamed in cumin-infused broth, and *murgh mussalam*, poussin with Kashmiri chillies and browned onions. Downstairs is Akbar, much more than just a restaurant cocktail lounge.

DELHI STAR

28 **Rasoi Vineet Bhatia**
14 10 Lincoln Street

Delhi-trained chef Vineet Bhatia brought the status of Indian food up a notch with Zaika, where he earned the place a Michelin star in 2001, the first ever for an Indian chef. It was an accomplishment he set out to achieve since arriving in London in 1993 as a trained chef and finding the state of Indian cooking here rather disappointing. In 2004 he left Zaika and moved to these premises, where the rooms are more intimate, the décor more luscious, and the menu resembling poetry. Once on the plate, the choices aren't any less lyrical. The name translates to 'Vineet Bhatia's kitchen', and it is proudly a family operation, with Bhatia's wife Rashima running the dining room, which only seats thirty-five. Upstairs, two small private dining rooms are available, one of which includes a roof terrace. Bhatia claims to have accomplished his dream in having his own restaurant in which to continue refining and experimenting with his native cuisine. You can also enjoy his cooking on British Airways First or Business Class flights.

70 **St John**

28 26 St John Street

Located a stone's throw from Smithfield Market, where livestock was traded for some 200 years, St John is a symbol of the British love affair with meat. This association, according to Trevor Gulliver, who started the restaurant with chef Fergus Henderson in 1994, happened somewhat by accident. True, one of the most famous and photographed items on their menu is bone marrow served with toasted flat bread and parsley salad, but this is more a reflection of the quality of the cuisine than a commitment to meat-eating. But St John also prides itself on its relationship with farmer-producers. Their fresh-baked bread can be bought from the bakery, and the fact that they butcher their own meat gives them the opportunity and, they feel, an obligation to use all the parts. With a staunchly loyal following that includes dozens who ask for the menu to be faxed to them daily (some just so they can find out when tripe is being served), it is not hard to be won over by Gulliver's belief that 'a good restaurant is like a good friend'. The stark, white-washed premises – which included a former smokehouse – complement the food perfectly.

With a television documentary chronicling the daily grind of running his own restaurant in pursuit of at least one Michelin star, Tom Aikens seemed to run the risk of eclipsing his own gastronomic achievements with the entertainment value of personal struggle. But no need to worry. Though we may have seen one too many kitchen-confidential shows, what Aikens really dishes out is worth talking about. From the black-painted façade on a Chelsea side street to the crisply white-clad waiters and simple floral displays, the feeling is one of serene sophistication. Of course, the menu follows suit, promising things that sound only mildly exotic but tempting enough and delivering a range of carefully crafted flavours that give credence to that Michelin rating. Choose duck foie gras and fig purée followed by turbot with langoustine ravioli or, if you're feeling more adventurous, the lauded braised pig's head with pork belly and stuffed trotter, and prepare for a memorable experience all around.

drink

When people think of London, they think of pubs. And while there are beautiful and characterful public houses throughout the city, those of great individual style are rare but well worth a detour. Today, however, pubs are only part of the story. Fuelled by London's famed club culture, its status as a magnet in the global design scene and more relaxed laws on drinking hours, chic watering holes are establishing themselves everywhere. After a couple of centuries of tea hegemony, coffee culture has re-entered London life, with delightful cafés popping up in neighbourhoods everywhere. Whether you're in the mood for a sleek lounge, a funky DJ dance-bar or an oak-panelled medieval pub, read on.

A NEW WORLD OF TEA

14 | **Tea Palace**

26 | 175 Westbourne Grove

Tara Calcraft opened the Tea Palace and began sourcing
teas from around the globe because, she says, 'there's a
whole world of tea, from black to green, oolong to white',
that most of us don't know about, and because she thinks
that, in the UK at least, people drink mostly poor quality
tea on a daily basis. Offering everything from a fine Earl
Grey to special hand-tied Chinese teas either by the cup
or sold in their distinctive packaging, the café also serves
brunch and lunch in addition to the traditional afternoon
or Champagne teas.

Oliver Peyton, restaurateur founder of such swanky London establishments as The Admiralty (p. 55) and Isola has gone one better with Inn the Park, a stylish restaurant set in the bucolic beauty of St James's Park, overlooking the duck pond and just a stone's throw from Buckingham Palace. The building by architect Michael Hopkins and interior by Tom Dixon remind visitors that they are in one of the most design-conscious cities in the world. Good for high-quality British food or just a drink outside or up on the roof terrace.

42 **The Portrait Restaurant**

The National Portrait Gallery has always been one of London's must-see museums, but a recent extension and refurbishment has given it one of the best views in London. On top of the new Ondaatje wing, just behind the National Gallery on Trafalgar Square, the gallery's rooftop restaurant has magnificent views across London – the ideal place for an afternoon tea or late afternoon cocktail. With Nelson's Column rising up from a roofscape of white and verdigris domes, and Big Ben in the distance, the true drama of London's architecture is revealed in full.

84 **Vertigo42**

For security reasons, you'll need to call in advance (one day for lunch, three weeks for evening drinks) to enjoy one of the most breathtaking views of London while sipping Champagne. Curvy, bright-blue, swivelling armchairs take full advantage of the vistas from the 42nd floor, atop the tallest building in the City of London. Although the bar serves mainly Champagne – thirty varieties at last count – there is a selection of wines as well as oysters, lobster, caviar and sushi. You pay for the view, but it's hard to imagine a better way to do so.

FASHIONABLE SCENE

28 **Blue Bar**

29 The Berkeley Hotel, Wilton Place

A new take on the hotel bar, sensuously reimagined by designer David Collins, the Blue Bar takes the Regency interior to a new level of chic. Vivid blue – what Collins calls 'Lutyens blue' – and a white onyx bar and crocodile-leather print floor set the scene, with bull's-eye mirrors, Art Déco-style chairs and tasselled hanging lamps adding appropriate flourishes. Reflecting surfaces shine, as does the sparkling service. The cocktail selection, served with honeyed nuts, is civilized – no silly concoctions – mainly Martinis, Champagne cocktails and grown-up drinks.

DRIPPING WITH HISTORY

42 **Gordon's Wine Bar**

51 47 Villiers Street

If there ever was a truly down-to-earth wine bar, Gordon's is it. From 1364 it was a warehouse for cargoes of sherry and port coming off the busy River Thames. Its origins as a wine bar date from around 1870, and it has been in the hands of its current owner for more than thirty years. Today, you can still enjoy a glass of one of eighty wines in the subterranean medieval vaults that literally drip with ambience. The incomparable interiors, teeming with loyal customers (especially after work), bring alive another time that couldn't be re-created anywhere else.

The Mitre's history goes back to 1546 when it was built by Bishop Goodrich for the servants of Ely Palace. The palace appears in Shakespeare's *Richard II*, Dr Johnson is said to have visited the tavern itself, and today you can still see the trunk of a cherry tree around which Queen Elizabeth I is said to have danced on May Day. Probably the most attractive pub in London – and the hardest to find – the Mitre's small rooms and dark-wood panelling retain a pub atmosphere almost impossible to find elsewhere: no music, just the pleasing din of people chatting.

84 The Blackfriar

4 174 Queen Victoria Street

Built on the site of a Dominican monastery that is today a rather unprepossessing concrete traffic interchange, the only Art Nouveau pub in a city dominated by Victoriana is an unexpected delight. Just across the Thames from the Tate Modern (p. 101), the fantastic marble and gold-mosaiced 19th-century interior is largely overlooked, despite its curious and intimate 'grotto' (carved from a railway vault). The interior flourishes are made more appealing by the pub's pleasingly unprecious nature, as if it supposed all places should be like this.

WINE IN TRANSIT

70 Smithy's

4 15–17 Leeke Street

Off the busy, gritty travel hub of King's Cross, on a narrow cobblestoned alley in an emerging warehouse area, Smithy's barely makes itself known, but the unassuming exterior conceals one of the capital's most atmospheric wine bars. What used to be a 19th-century horse-drawn bus garage is the setting for a huge selection of wines by the glass or bottle, with light bar meals to soak up any excess. As the area around King's Cross is regenerating, so has a new owner at Smithy's tidied it up a bit, but the place's old character retains its charm.

PLEASING DECAY
14 **Windsor Castle**
32 114 Campden Hill Road

There's simply no modern way to create an interior that exudes the welcoming, gently time-worn ambience of the Windsor Castle, built in 1828, which appears to have remained virtually untouched for almost two centuries. Far from feeling rarefied, the pub – once an inn – seems as though it's always been an integral part of the quiet residential area in which it's set. While the deep wood atmosphere warms in winter, a large tree-shaded garden invites pleasurable drinking in summer. A place for quiet conversation or contemplation, whatever the season.

SHABBY GENTILITY
28 **Anglesea Arms**
8 15 Selwood Terrace

Just north of the shopping highway that is the Fulham Road, the Anglesea Arms sits in quiet repose, offering a welcoming embrace with outdoor tables in leafy shadows and a discreet period air that bespeaks the days when it was presented as a gift to Lady Joseph from her husband, Sir Maxwell Joseph. This is a pub whose early Victorian charms are well preserved, along with decorative details, such as framed old photographs and historic engravings, shaded chandeliers and velvet swag draperies that provide a reliably pleasing encounter every time.

The Albion

6 10 Thornhill Road

The Albion has had a rather rough journey over the last few years, going from a comfortable place for a pint in a relaxed and friendly atmosphere to a bit of a demise as part of a group holdings pub. But these days, The Albion seems to have a new lease of life. Yes, the décor has been modernized and stripped down, but the garden has been broadened and brought back to life and the interior made welcoming again, despite losing some of its Victoriana. The menu has been revamped as well, and offers traditional English fare, including roasted suckling pig.

PINTS IN THE PASSAGE

70 **The Elk in the Woods**

15 39 Camden Passage

The pedestrian Camden Passage (p. 77) has become a magnet for chic boutiques and funky cafés in recent years. The Elk in the Woods was one of the first of the more groovy bars to migrate toward this quieter side of Upper Street, and over the last few years has established itself as one of the hipper places to drink of an evening. While the out-of-town crowds swarm the chain pubs on the main drag, enjoy a more civilized pint at the lead-lined bar or in the rustic wood-lined lounge. The music is changeable, but never too intrusive for conversation.

WILD NIGHT

58 **Crazy Bear**

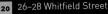

20 26–28 Whitfield Street

Cowhide upholstery, leather-covered walls in cavernous alcoves, shimmering coppery surfaces and a smashing list of cocktails bring a buzz to this basement bar that keeps regulars and newcomers streaming down the stairs. The front is knowingly unmarked, except perhaps by the doorman. An impressive list of single-malt and blended whiskies, vodkas, aperitifs, sakes, gins and rums and drinks to mix them in keeps the bartenders on their toes and the guests in their seats.

Named after the brothels that were once sought out by sailors in port, not completely without meaning in this area of King's Cross, the Ruby Lounge has accomplished the somewhat contradictory task of making a run-down area more inviting. Along the ramshackle collection of improving and crumbling shopfronts, the Ruby Lounge's glowing red logo outside and breathtaking Verner Panton chandelier and wall lights inside are welcome signs in the night. The music is groovy, as are the people.

From its origins as a migrating Sunday afternoon dance club to one of the happiest venues in the West End, The Social is a product of the Heavenly record- and club producers, whose parties have seen some of London's most famous DJs. In 1999, David Adjaye, architect of choice for London's Brit Artists, remodelled the interiors using unconventional exterior materials to create a two-level space that allows for all variety of dance activity. Add to that exceptionally clued-in music and a joyful crowd, and you've found your haven.

Under the arches of the Kingsland Viaduct, Cargo has taken on the ambitious task of providing restaurant, bar and club beneath a series of vaulted roofs and making them all seem very cool. With its vague dockside theme, the branded Cargo logo greets you but that is the only given here. The open dining area is filled with giant square wood tables and views out to the planted courtyard garden. Music is one of the principal draws, with regular performances and internationally renowned DJs making the scene.

New bars come and go, but in this area of Notting Hill a new venue that is trendy but friendly, noteworthy but welcoming is something to be pleased about. Sitting a mere stone's throw from the Electric Cinema (p. 19) and in the heart of the market shopping district, Trailer Happiness offers a comfortable kitschy atmosphere with tropical-themed décor and drinks to match. Its trailer-home vibe and cocktails, created by drinks guru Jonathan Downey (who launched the Matchbar), attract interested locals and hipsters alike.

Within the last decade Hoxton Square has become synonymous with hip arts and crafts studios during the daytime and groovy bars at night, largely supplanting Soho as a night-time destination. Inevitably many of the creatives who made the area what it is have moved on – but the vibe remains intact, if made up more of visitors than of locals. Interestingly, most of the places that formed the early nightlife are still there, and still draw a crowd. Slightly off the square, a large, minimally furnished space

with plate-glass windows, aglow with neon, announces what used to be electricity showrooms but has for the last several years been one of the area's principal watering holes. With a prominent but not prepossessing position on the southwest corner of Hoxton Square is Bluu, formerly the Blue Note club, which many would argue was the epicentre of drum 'n' bass dance music. Five years later it features a modern stainless-steel-trimmed interior and DJs who continue the tradition of its predecessor. Next door and down one level, this time lacking in signage, is the Hoxton Square Bar & Kitchen, another of the area's standbys. The open interior, set slightly below ground level, is animated at night by the eerie sensation of car headlights as they turn just before the bar. A few blocks away is Liquid, a small but vividly coloured venue that comes alive at night. Heading somewhat south to Great Eastern Street are Medicine Bar and the Great Eastern Dining Rooms, which in addition to its bar and downstairs lounge serves respectable pan-Asian food.

shop

Like most metropolises, London is a hive of commercial activity, buzzing with grand department stores, stylish international-label outlets and off-beat boutiques. At the other end of the style spectrum are the dozens of street markets where real Londoners sell everything from antiques to country produce. Energized by the capital's renowned design schools, boutiques and speciality shops are springing up around the city – but are often off the beaten track. To understand what London style is all about, you need to seek out the individualists who keep London on the global fashion map. For classic British labels or unheard-of street-chic upstarts, here is a guide.

42 **Dover Street Market**

18 17–18 Dover Street

The style makeover of Dover Street started in many ways with the arrival of this retail space in 2004. Dover Street Market, five sparsely furnished floors of avant-garde international labels under one roof, was the brainchild of Franco-Japanese designer Rei Kawakubo. Designer concessions are arranged on each floor in discreet sections, with edgy works of art punctuating bare concrete spaces. Harder-to-find British brands are here, too: this is one of the few places, for example, that you can buy Olivia Morris shoes, rather than making an appointment with the designer herself. In 2006 Kawakubo staged a retrospective of Stephen Jones Millinery here. If you can't find anything to suit your taste among Comme des Garçons, Véronique Branquinho, John Galliano, Pierre Hardy, and a concession of East End cult favourite Labour and Wait (p. 91), you can get a DSM T-shirt out of one of the store vending machines. There is also a small café area on the top floor run by the Rose Bakery.

NO FLOUNCES HERE

58 Margaret Howell

6 34 Wigmore Street

Margaret Howell is one of the best-known names in the British fashion industry, though she gets press for her understated elegance rather than for flashy couture. She doesn't do flouncy or flowery, but rather dresses women who don't mind a bit of (unstructured) masculine: cuffed trousers and striped (oversized) shirts, herringbone jackets and narrow skirts. They're all given nice feminine touches and, of course, fine quality fabrics and tailoring. Howell does menswear, too, with great aplomb. This, her flagship store, is where you'll find the fullest range of her smart, practical and beautifully cut designs.

- Harvie & Hudson, nos 96–97
- Dunhill, no. 48
- J. Floris, no. 89
- Turnbull & Asser, nos 71–72

The street of men's shirtmakers is a must-see for anyone looking to procure the genuine English article, from shoes to shirts. Harvie & Hudson, which was founded in 1929, is at nos 96–97, and even if their traditional style is not to your liking, the fine Victorian shopfront is worth the short walk from any of the numerous establishments. Dunhill, now available worldwide, started out as Alfred Dunhill the tobacconist before becoming the global purveyor of fine menswear and accessories it is today, now with a decidedly modern edge. Provisions of a different sort are available at J. Floris, the oldest perfumer in London, established as a barber shop in 1730 by Juan Famenias Floris of Menorca. The shop's interior is bejeweled with bottled essences, candles, soaps and lotions, some displayed in the Spanish mahogany cabinets that were obtained from the Great Exhibition of 1851. For bespoke shirts, it must be Turnbull & Asser, probably the street's best-known shop and supplier to the Prince of Wales. Fine mother-of-pearl buttons, specially woven Sea Island cotton, 'the most gentlemanly of shirtings', and broad, three-buttoned cuffs are among Turnbull & Asser's trademarks.

Even on the most famous street for men's bespoke tailoring in the world times have changed, and the prevailing trend to modernize classics is influencing the look on Savile Row. Led by innovators such as Ozwald Boateng, a younger generation of tailors are beginning to seize control. Amid the traditional shops are edgier talents, such as Richard James, who has attracted a younger clientele with his modern cuts and banned advertisements. Anderson & Sheppard, where British fashion star Alexander McQueen (p. 173) cut his cloth as a teenager, are perhaps best known for dressing royalty, and William Hunt's sartorial flair has won him a number of music-world clients. Kilgour traces its roots back to 1882 and has suited up the likes of Fred Astaire and Cary Grant; under new management a sleek, modern approach to ready-to-wear tailoring has emerged with these equally sleek shop floors opening in 2007. Up the road, Gieves & Hawkes has also undergone some updating as creative director James Whishow (previously of Calvin Klein) created younger label Gieves and brought in a trendier but still demanding clientele.

42 **John Lobb**

23 88 Jermyn Street

A Cornish farm boy who learned the bootmaking craft, John Lobb received a royal warrant for his work from the Prince of Wales, later Edward VII. Today the company holds three royal warrants from the Queen, the Duke of Edinburgh and the current Prince of Wales. The shop is a shrine to craftsmanship, as John Lobb still specialize in and have become almost synonymous with the art of the hand-made shoe. Each pair is numbered and fitted with its own shoe trees. Buckskin, satin calf and ostrich are just some of the leathers available.

THE NEW CLASSIC

42 **Paul Smith**

47 40–44 Floral Street

Starting out as a gopher in a clothing warehouse at eighteen, Paul Smith has gone on to become probably England's best-known menswear designer. He was one of the first to take classic cuts of men's suits and insert bold details or design a truly well-made men's shirt with a bright contemporary pattern. Though he now has an international reputation, designs for women and children and has developed his brand to include home accessories and objects (see Paul Smith Curiosity Shop; p. 48), this remains the base for his signature men's fashions.

EXOTIC ESSENCES
42 **Ormonde Jayne**
25 The Royal Arcade, 28 Old Bond Street

Even if you weren't interested in the exotic scents wafting from its shelves, you would stop and notice this jewel-box shop with its antique gold shagreen wallcovering, black glass chandeliers, and the array of primly positioned red boxes with their perfect black bows. Against the smoked glass and black lacquer wall display there are also candles, flowers and rows of bottles, all promising a one-of-a-kind scent experience. Founder Linda Pilkington began her career in scent by growing and selling her own flowers, making scented candles and bathing oils and scented cushions for gifts. After travelling the world for fourteen years gathering experience in retail and exotic oils and essences, she returned to London in 2002 to set up Ormonde Jayne Perfumery, which she says, is 'a return to the golden age of perfumery'. To date, Pilkington offers ten perfumes: of these, Orris Noir, named for the black iris of Amman and carrying notes of davana, pink pepper and iris and a base containing myrrh, patchouli and gaiac, is probably the most beguiling.

PATTERN PRODIGIES

42 **Eley Kishimoto**

42 27 Greek Street

Eley Kishimoto has become one of the hottest names in London fashion, being both known to the fashion-aware and yet unknown, as so little about them has been publicized. Mark Eley and his Japanese wife, Wakako Kishimoto, both trained in England. Previously located in a former jam factory in Bermondsey, which served as their workshop, factory and only public showroom (though their designs are sold through other outlets worldwide), the duo recently moved to these premises in Soho. Known for their unique printed designs, which are mostly hand-drawn by Kishimoto and applied to everything from textiles to luggage to wallpaper, the two got their start producing patterns for top designers such as Alexander McQueen (p. 173), Nicole Farhi and Hussein Chalayan. They then began staging their own ready-to-wear collections twice a year, and have been consistently successful with their striking designs that border tantalizingly on the kitsch. Accessible to more than just the fashion élite, they are certainly set for bigger things, so get them while you can.

MARKET FASHION

14 **Preen**

5 5 Portobello Green

The British design team of Justin Thornton and Thea Bregazzi had a popular following even before they settled in this diminutive space off Portobello Road. Several years after establishing themselves here, they have, rather strangely, remained, despite acres of coverage in the fashion press and highly lauded catwalk shows nearly every season. Originally wowing crowds with puffed and quilted numbers that had a certain edgy glamour, they continue to experiment with shapes, textures and patterns to create fashions that are uniquely their own.

VINTAGE STREET

14 **Rellik**

3 8 Golborne Road

Located in edgy Ladbroke Grove opposite Myro Goldfinger's brutalist triumph (or terror, some might say), Trellik Tower, Rellik is a second-hand shop with a difference, as its loyal customers and fashion-magazine editors are well aware. Three former Portobello Road stall owners set up shop to offer select vintage wear from the 1920s onward, each with her own area of speciality, including both ready-to-wear and couture pieces. If you look hard enough, you just might just find a classic Westwood outfit.

84 Lara Bohinc 107
51 Hoxton Square

Cameron Diaz, Björk, Lucy Liu and Sarah Jessica Parker are among the A-list celebrities who have fallen under the spell of Lara Bohinc's cutting-edge, but distinctly feminine jewelry pieces. Until recently, Bohinc's creations were available only through large luxury retailers, but in 2004 the young Slovenian-born designer opened her only shop in the creative hub of Hoxton Square (see also p. 159). Now her collections 'Drops', inspired by the designs of the 1920s and 1930s, 'Ovals', a new take on modern classics, and 'Curb', which draws on the hip-hop urban influences, are all available in one space.

14 Pippa Small
11 Colville Mews

Jewelry designer Pippa Small originally studied medical anthropology, travelling in far-flung corners of the globe to pursue her research. She later developed her own jewelry designs, working with Chloé, Nicole Farhi, and Tom Ford for Gucci, and collaborated on a fair-trade basis with many indigenous groups to help them maintain their traditional crafts. In this precious boutique only a few steps from the sweeping fashions of Alice Temperley (p. 172), she presents her own work 'inspired by rough minerals, rocks and plant life, as well as ancient and classical designs', using 'uncut gems and unusual crystals'.

Irishman Philip Treacy's approach to millinery is that of a sculptor. He staged the first catwalk show of his own designs in 1993 with the help of supermodels Christy Turlington, Kate Moss and Naomi Campbell. But Treacy's designs are worth the attention on their own, whether it's a pale-pink top hat set off with a giant silk rose, a proliferation of green leaves sprouting from a headband, or a delicate swirl perched atop a well-groomed forehead. And while he designs for some of the most exclusive customers, he also makes a not-so-haute range, available in this shop, that lesser mortals can enjoy.

Westbourne Grove is chock-a-block with designer boutiques, but this gem of a bespoke jewelry shop is slightly removed from the fray. Despite the ruby-red front, it doesn't announce itself, and though you are welcome to drop in, you must make an appointment if you want a consultation with the lady herself. Having worked for costume jewelers Butler & Wilson (p. 32), Azagury-Partridge is one of Britain's most inventive jewelry designers, and her bold, baroque creations in 18-carat yellow, white and rose gold and platinum are full of shape, colour and wit.

DISCREET BOUTIQUE

14 Alice Temperley

 6–10 Colville Mews

She has been compared to a waif, a sprite, all manner of elf-like forest-dwelling creatures, and this is probably not only to do with her youth and lissome figure, but with her light-mannered feminine, flowing creations. Having built a fashion empire at the tender age of thirty, Alice Temperley has created a retail space that is as welcoming as her clothes are captivating. The wood flooring of the old mews building has been polished up but left looking rustic, making a nice earthy contrast to the bright hues and soft drapery of the pieces on display. Her signature dresses are finely gathered and flowing, with fanning waistlines in fabrics that drape like Grecian wraps. But Temperley is not only about whispery tea dresses: her autumn/winter 2007/8 collection was inspired by 'Paris in the 1900s' and the Ballet Russes, and also harks back to 1960s London with short black skirts and crop jackets. Temperley also offers a bridal service here.

42
Alexander McQueen
19 4–5 Old Bond Street

Once the bad boy of British fashion, Alexander McQueen is now one of the world's leading fashion designers. After a five-year stint as chief designer for Givenchy, he turned his focus to his own label, opening his exclusive shops and developing menswear and eyeglasses lines, and a signature fragrance. This shop, opened in 2003 (the year he was awarded a CBE), is a dynamic backdrop to the visual and textural excitement that is McQueen's trademark and has won him a list of celebrity clients.

42
Stella McCartney
15 30 Bruton Street

This shop is as beautifully detailed as the designer's own creations: the Georgian townhouse has been restored with grand spaces and period elements lightened up with a glass-covered atrium leading to the shoe room, where the sexy-funky footwear features the label 'suitable for vegetarians'. Wood floors, a dainty woodland-motif wall covering, plum-coloured carpet leading up a spiral stair to more airy rooms, and a boudoir space hung with lingerie and dotted with jewel-like perfume bottles is an enchanting display that doesn't upstage the items on sale.

 28
David Mellor

16 4 Sloane Square

David Mellor operates on the simple principle that well-designed equipment can improve your life. Mellor, Royal Designer for Industry, has an international reputation. He has always specialized in metalwork and has often been described as 'the cutlery king'. Mellor opened his Sloane Square shop in 1969, and today it sells his own range of tableware and a large selection of kitchen accessories, as well as his cutlery range in silver plate and stainless steel, all manufactured in England.

ART DÉCO EXTRAORDINAIRE

58 **Gallery 1930/Susie Cooper Ceramics**

1 18 Church Street

Probably London's most comprehensive collection of Art Déco ceramics, furniture and lighting is housed in a small but richly filled shop on a road that is like a secret hoard of antiques dealers. Geoffrey Peake and Nick Jones first set up shop at Alfie's, a collection of dealers' stalls, as Susie Cooper Ceramics, selling mostly the work of the 'quintessentially English designer'. Here in their own premises they offer a wide collection of 1930s pieces, including boldly patterned Clarice Cliff vessels and solid-hued Keith Murray designs for Wedgwood.

14
Melt

24 59 Ledbury Road

The cool, white shop reminds you slightly of one of Willy Wonka's laboratory rooms, though much more tasteful and modern. However the lab, of sorts, is right in the back where you might see master chocolatier Keith Hurdman, who holds the prestigious Truffe d'Or as Swiss Champion Confectioner/Chocolatier, working on another batch of award-winning morsels (he won a double gold at the World Chocolate Awards 2007). Some of his award-winners are available in the beautifully arranged selections on display. Also look for the shop's series of chocolates made in collaboration with London's top chefs.

retreat

It is probably true that the real England is to be found in the country, not in the cities. And though the regions immediately surrounding London's concrete jungle are in many ways bucolic translations of the city sensibility, it is not hard to find pockets that feel worlds away, even though some are a mere thirty minutes by train from the metropolitan centre. These four getaways represent very different experiences, but each is distinctly English and an ideal tonic after an intoxicating few days in the urban buzz.

Brighton: Seaside Hip

- Blanch House
- Hotel Pelirocco
- The Royal Pavilion

Formerly the playground of Regency royals and today a hip seaside clubbing destination, Brighton is the quintessential English getaway, particularly for the youthfully inclined. Dynamized by students from the local university, one of the liveliest nightclub scenes in the the UK, if not Europe, this recreation destination is just over an hour from London. An unusually high concentration of record and jewelry shops, quarters of narrow pedestrianized lanes and the wide-open boardwalk unite in a cool concoction of kitsch, fun, craft and decadence.

The town centre has four principal quarters: North Laine, a tight grid of quaint, brightly coloured houses with lively boutiques and bars; the Lanes, a rabbit warren of even narrower alleyways packed with clothes shops and jewelers; the Seafront, which features a boardwalk and the Arches, a long colonnade comprising mainly restaurants and bars, many of which turn into nightclubs when day becomes night; and Kemp Town, east of the pier, between St James Street and Marina Drive, with a more relaxed vibe. At opposite ends of the action are two hotels whose character fits perfectly with the Brighton scene. The intimate Blanch House in Kemp Town is a delightful twelve-room hotel owned by Amanda Blanch and Chris Edwardes, with each room quirkily themed and cleverly decorated; its small restaurant serves contemporary British. Hotel Pelirocco, on Regency Square, is all rock 'n' roll: Playstations in every room, idiosyncratic decoration and a host of guests from London's music scene have garnered the hotel international attention and a colourful following.

For a relatively small town, there is a high concentration of shops, over 300 at last count, many of which are independently owned and feature a broad spectrum of wares, from streetwear and locally designed crafts to 1970s furniture and decorative objects, to kites and beachwear – with prices generally noticeably lower than their London counterparts. Do not miss the Royal Pavilion, a faux-exotic pleasure palace built by the then Prince of Wales (later George IV) in 1785 and an entirely appropriate symbol of the town's exuberance and excess.

Bath and Babington House: Georgian Splendour, Contemporary Style
near Frome, Somerset

Londoners have been going to Bath for rest and rejuvenation probably since the Romans first exploited the natural hot springs. But it was at the height of its popularity as a retreat for the fashionable rich during the 18th century, when English architect John Wood and his son (also John Wood) created the elegant neoclassical squares and crescents using golden Bath stone, making it one of the most picturesque cities in England – today just over an hour by train from London. The city's heart is the convergence of the Abbey Church (1616), the Roman Baths and Museum and the Pump Room, a grand tearoom that gives something of the flavour of Bath society popularized by Jane Austen. In the elevated northwest near the park and botanic gardens, the Royal Crescent is a masterpiece of 18th-century architecture.

Restaurants and lodgings are abundant in Bath, but a stylish and fitting base is just a few miles away, near Frome, in the early Georgian country estate of Babington House, where 18th-century charm and modern convenience have been married to fruitful success. Nick Jones, the enterprising figure behind Soho House and the refurbished Electric Cinema (p. 19) in London, has brought modern comforts – such as a heated outdoor swimming pool, a cinema, clubby bar (try the house Champagne cocktail or hot toddy) and gourmet restaurant – to a discerning urban crowd and nestled them comfortably in the arms of this grand country house. Drawing rooms with furniture by contemporary designers and rustic-chic room décor that respect the architecture have transformed the manor house into a very singular environment. With gym and spa facilities housed in a former cowshed overlooking the two lap pools, the picture is complete. Everything is perfectly in keeping with Bath's history as a place of high fashion: there is nothing that Georgian aristocrats wouldn't expect to find were they cavorting here in the 21st century. The large, light-filled breakfast room offers meals almost any time of day and the restaurant delivers high-quality dishes that take full advantage of local and organic produce.

Bray: An Epicurean Destination

- The Waterside Inn
- The Fat Duck
- The Hind's Head
- Monkey Island Hotel

A mere thirty-minute train journey from Paddington station takes you to one of the highest concentrations of Michelin stars in the country, set in the verdant Thames-side setting of Bray, a 16th-century village. Just a few minutes apart, The Waterside Inn and The Fat Duck, both in converted country pubs, have set the highest standards in culinary excellence – in completely different ways.

The Waterside Inn was opened by Albert and Michel Roux, the brothers who in 1967 redefined London's world of gastronomy with the opening of Le Gavroche. Today Michel and his son Alain, who recently assumed the helm to rave reviews, run The Waterside Inn with the élan and elegance that have made it another modern institution. Despite the excellence of the food and service, the converted pub surroundings and dining room overlooking the river impart a notably unstuffy air – formality softened by countryside.

Pursuing excellence in a very different manner, The Fat Duck is the product of Heston Blumenthal. Since opening the restaurant in 1995, he has explored innovative modes of cooking that draw on science rather than conventional kitchen methods. His intensive research into chemistry, psychology and sensory perception – an approach sometimes referred to as 'molecular gastronomy', although Blumenthal refutes this term – has uncovered an unexpected spectrum of tastes, moods and memories that are a revolution in cooking. More recently, Blumenthal has applied his chemical wizardry to classic pub-style comfort food at the nearby Hind's Head, an ideal alternative for those seeking a less formal meal in warm surroundings.

After such splendid dining experiences, you will want nothing more than to fall asleep to the sound of the Thames lapping against its banks. For those too sated to move, The Waterside Inn offers ten rooms in the main house and outbuildings around the site. On a tiny Thames island close to both restaurants, the peaceful Monkey Island Hotel is an historic property accessed only by a pedestrian bridge. Most of its twenty-six rooms have river or garden views.

WATERSIDE

ELIZABETHAN BOLTHOLE

Gravetye Manor:
The Quintessential Country House Experience

near East Grinstead, West Sussex

Less than thirty miles south of London, a thousand acres of forest are the setting for one of the southeast's most luxurious country house hotels. After a fifty-minute train ride from central London you arrive in the Sussex town of East Grinstead; a further short taxi drive takes you through green countryside to historic Gravetye Manor. Built in 1598 by Richard Infield for his wife, Katherine, the stone mansion retains most of its Elizabethan elements, despite periods of neglect. Some of the windows are still ornamented with delicate wrought-iron glazing bars and open to the expanse of gardens and fields that were tamed and encouraged by the renowned English landscape gardener, William Robinson.

Robinson bought the manor and the surrounding land in 1884 and lived there until he died in 1935, laying out the gardens of small plants and flowers, trees and shrubs, and pioneering what became known as the English 'natural' style. The arrangement of the gardens is his living legacy and no small part of the appeal of Gravetye, which was bought by Peter Herbert and converted to a hotel in 1958.

The interiors are enchanting. Warm rooms, printed English fabrics, period portraits and flowers, as well as service that is informal but highly discreet and attentive, make guests feel truly welcome in an atmosphere of old-world luxury. Two wood-panelled drawing rooms, each with a well-tended wood-burning fire, can be used by guests for quiet reading, relaxing or for having tea or drinks. The restaurant, led by chef Mark Raffan, has earned a Michelin star, so requires booking ahead. Around lunch you might consider a walk through the countryside to the rustic pub of a neighbouring village.

Rooms are finely decorated in traditional English style, even with the occasional ceiling or floor slant that is so much part of the character of this cherished old property. Peter and Susan Herbert strive to maintain an air that is 'not trendy, but at the same time not aged and stuffy'. Their forty years of experience with the house and the clientele ensure that their delightful establishment will continue for many years.

contact

All telephone numbers are given for dialling locally: the country code for England is 44; the city code for London 20. Calling from abroad, therefore, one dials (+44 20) plus the number given below. Telephone numbers in the retreat section are given for dialling from London; if calling from abroad, dial the country code (44) and drop the 0 at the start of the number. The number in brackets by the name is the page number on which the entry appears.

202 [23]
202 Westbourne Grove
London W11 2RH
T 7727 2722
W www.nicolefarhi.com

Acorn House [73]
69 Swinton Street
London WC1X 9NT
T 7812 1842
E info@acornhouserestaurant.com
W www.acornhouserestaurant.com

Adam Street [135]
9 Adam Street
London WC2N 6AA
T 7379 8000
E reception@adamstreet.co.uk
W www.adamstreet.co.uk

The Admiralty [55]
Somerset House, Strand
London WC2R 1LA
T 7845 4646
E info@theadmiraltyrestaurant.com
W www.theadmiraltyrestaurant.com

The Albion [155]
10 Thornhill Road
London N1 1HW
T 7607 7450

Alexander McQueen [173]
4–5 Old Bond Street
London W1S 4PD
T 7355 0088
W www.alexandermcqueen.com

Alice Temperley [172]
6–10 Colville Mews
London W11 2DA
T 7229 7957
W www.temperleylondon.com

Ally Capellino [91]
9 Calvert Avenue
London E2 7JP
T 7613 3073
E shop@allycapellino.co.uk
W www.allycapellino.co.uk

Almeida Theatre [73]
Almeida Street
London N1 1TA
T 7359 4404
E info@almeida.co.uk
W www.almeida.co.uk

Anchor & Hope [102]
36 The Cut
London SE1 8LP
T 7928 9898
E anchorandhope@btconnect.com

Anderson & Sheppard [165]
32 Old Burlington Street
London W1S 3AT
T 7734 1420
E office@anderson-sheppard.co.uk
W www.anderson-sheppard.co.uk

Andrew Edmonds [51]
46 Lexington Street
London W1R 3LH
T 7437 5708

Anglesea Arms [154]
15 Selwood Terrace
London SW7 3QG
T 7373 7960

Annie's [77]
12 Camden Passage
London N1 8ED
T 7359 0796

Antoni & Alison [80]
43 Rosebery Avenue
London EC1R 4SH
T 7833 2141
E info@antoniandalison.co.uk
W www.antoniandalison.co.uk

Anya Hindmarch [37]
157–158 Sloane Street
London SW1X 9EH
T 7838 9177
W www.anyahindmarch.com

Arbutus [137]
63–64 Frith Street
London W1D 3JW
T 7734 4545
E info@arbutusrestaurant.co.uk
W www.arbutusrestaurant.co.uk

@Work [88]
156 Brick Lane
London E1 6RU
T 7377 0597
E joatworkgallery@aol.com
W www.atworkgallery.co.uk

Baby Ceylon [17]
12 Portobello Green
281 Portobello Road
London W10 5TZ
T 8968 9501
E info@babyceylon.com
W www.babyceylon.com

Baltic [101]
74 Blackfriars Road
London SE1 8HA
T 7928 1111
E info@balticrestaurant.co.uk
W www.balticrestaurant.co.uk

Bam-Bou [62]
1 Percy Street
London W1T 1DB
T 7323 9130
W www.bam-bou.co.uk

Ben Day [88]
18 Hanbury Street
London E1 6QR
T 7247 9977
E info@benday.co.uk
W www.benday.co.uk

Ben de Lisi [37]
40 Elizabeth Street
London SW1W 9NZ
T 7730 2994
W www.bendelisi.com

Bermondsey Market [106]
Bermondsey Square
Long Lane and Bermondsey Street
London SE1

Bibendum Oyster Bar [31]
Michelin House, 81 Fulham Road
London SW3 6RD
T 7581 5817
E reservations@bibendum.co.uk
W www.bibendum.co.uk

Bill Amberg [20]
21–22 Chepstow Corner
London W2 4XE
T 7727 3560
W www.billamberg.com

Bistrotheque [94]
23–27 Wadeson Street
London E2 9DR
T 8983 7900
E info@bistrotheque.com
W www.bistrotheque.com

The Blackfriar [153]
174 Queen Victoria Street
London EC4V 4EG
T 7236 5474

Blenheim Books [20]
11 Blenheim Crescent
London W11 2EE
T 7792 0777
E sales@blenheimbooks.co.uk
W www.blenheimbooks.co.uk

Blue Bar [151]
The Berkeley Hotel, Wilton Place
London SW1X 7RL
T 7201 1680
E info@the-berkeley.co.uk
W www.the-berkeley.co.uk

Bluu Bar [159]
1 Hoxton Square
London N1 6NU
T 7613 2793
E hoxton@bluu.co.uk
W www.bluu.co.uk

Boiler House [88]
152 Brick Lane
London E1 6RU

Books for Cooks [20]
4 Blenheim Crescent
London W11 1NN
T 7221 1992
E info@booksforcooks.com
W www.booksforcooks.com

Borough Market [106]
Southwark Street
London SE1 1TL
T 7407 1002
E info@boroughmarket.org.uk
W www.boroughmarket.org.uk

Brick Lane Beigel Bake [88]
159 Brick Lane
London E1 6SB
T 7729 0616

Browns [44]
24–27 South Molton Street
London W1K 5RD
T 7514 0016
E southmoltonstreet@
   brownsfashion.com
W www.brownsfashion.com

Browns Focus [44]
38–39 South Molton Street
London W1K 5RN
T 7514 0063
E brownsfocus@
   brownsfashion.com
W www.brownsfashion.com

Burlington Arcade [49]
Piccadilly
London W1
W www.burlington-arcade.co.uk

Butler & Wilson [32]
189 Fulham Road
London SW3 6JN
T 7352 3045
E info@butlerandwilson.co.uk
W www.butlerandwilson.co.uk

Ca4la [93]
23 Pitfield Street
London N1 6HB
T 7490 0056
W www.ca4la.com

Cadogan London [118]
75 Sloane Street
London SW1X 9SG
T 7235 7141
E info@cadogan.com
W www.cadogan.com

Café 1001 [88]
1 Dray Walk
91 Brick Lane
London. E1 6QL
T 7247 9679
W www.cafe1001.co.uk

Canal [74]
42 Cross Street
London N1 2BA
T 7704 0222

Caramel [23]
54 Ledbury Road
London W11 2AG
T 7727 0906
E info@caramel-shop.co.uk
W www.caramel-shop.co.uk

Cargo [158]
3 Rivington Street
London EC2A 3AY
T 7739 3440
W www.cargo-london.com

Caroline Groves [61]
37 Chiltern Street
London W1U 7PW
T 7935 2329
E enquiries@carolinegroves.co.uk
W www.carolinegroves.co.uk

Cecconi's [47]
5A Burlington Gardens
London W1S 3EP
T 7434 1500
W www.cecconis.co.uk

The Charles Lamb [77]
16 Elia Street
London N1 8DE
T 7837 5040

Chelsea Physic Garden [35]
66 Royal Hospital Road
London SW3 4HS
T 7352 5646
E enquiries@
chelseaphysicgarden.co.uk
W www.chelseaphysicgarden.co.uk

Christ Church Spitalfields [91]
Commercial Street
London E1 6LY
T 7247 7202
E admin@
christchurchspitalfields.org.uk
W www.ccspitalfields.org

Cinch [51]
5 Newburgh Street
London W1V 1LH
T 7287 4941

Cinnamon Club [139]
30–32 Great Smith Street
London SW1P 3BU
T 7222 2555
E info@cinnamonclub.com
W www.cinnamonclub.com

Clerkenwell Music [79]
27 Exmouth Market
London EC1R 4QL
T 7833 9757
W www.clerkenwellmusic.co.uk

The Cloth Shop [17]
290 Portobello Road
London W10 5TE
T 8968 6001

Cockfighter of Bermondsey [106]
96 Bermondsey Street
London SE1 3UB
T 7357 6482

Coco de Mer [55]
23 Monmouth Street
London WC2H 9DD
T 7836 8882
E sales@coco-de-mer.co.uk
W www.coco-de-mer.co.uk

**Columbia Road Flower
Market** [94]
Columbia Road
London E2
E columbia_flower_market@
btinternet.com
W www.columbia-flower-market.
freewebspace.com

Contemporary Applied Arts [65]
2 Percy Street
London W1T 1DD
T 7436 2344
E sales@caa.org.uk
W www.caa.org.uk

Courtauld Institute of Art [55]
Somerset House, Strand
London WC2R 0RN
T 7848 2777
E sales@caa.org.uk
W www.courtauld.ac.uk

Couverture [32]
310 King's Road
London SW3 5UH
T 7795 1200
E info@couverture.co.uk
W www.couverture.co.uk

The Cow [138]
89 Westbourne Park Road
London W2 5QH
T 7221 0021

Cowshed [17]
119 Portland Road
London W11 4LN
T 7078 1944
W www.
cowshedclarendoncross.com

Crazy Bear [156]
26–28 Whitfield Street
London W1T 2RG
T 7631 0088
E enquiries@crazybear-
london.co.uk
W www.crazybeargroup.co.uk

The Cross [18]
141 Portland Road
London W11 4LR
T 7727 6760

Cross Street Gallery [74]
40 Cross Street
London N1 2BA
T 7226 8600
E enquiries@artforsale.co.uk
W www.artforsale.co.uk

The Crown [77]
116 Cloudesley Road
London N1 0EB
T 7837 7107
E crown.islington@fullers.co.uk

W www.fullers.co.uk

Cutler & Gross [38]
7 and 16 Knightsbridge Green
London SW1X 7QL
T 7590 9995
E info@cutlerandgross.co.uk
W www.cutlerandgross.co.uk

Daunt Books [61]
83 Marylebone High Street
London W1U 4QW
T 7224 2295
E marylebone@dauntbooks.co.uk
W www.dauntbooks.co.uk

David Mellor [174]
4 Sloane Square
London SW1W 8EE
T 7730 4259
E sales@davidmellordesign.co.uk
W www.davidmellordesign.com

Delfina [106]
50 Bermondsey Street
London SE1 3UD
T 7357 0244
E book@thedelfina.co.uk
W www.thedelfina.co.uk

Dennis Severs' House [87]
18 Folgate Street
London E1 6BX
T 7247 4013
E info@dennissevershouse.co.uk
W www.dennissevershouse.co.uk

Design Museum [106]
28 Shad Thames
London SE1 2YD
T 0870 909 9009
E info@designmuseum.org
W www.designmuseum.org

Designworks [52]
42–44 Broadwick Street
London W1F 7AE
T 7434 1968
E designworks@abahouse.co.uk
W www.designworkslondon.co.uk

The Dispensary [51]
9 Newburgh Street
London W1F 7RL
T 7287 8145
E info@thedispensary.net
W www.thedispensary.net

$ Grills & Martinis [79]
2 Exmouth Market
London EC1R 4PX
T 7278 0077

Donovan Bar [49]
Brown's Hotel, Albemarle Street
London W1S 4BP
T 7493 6020

Dover Castle [62]
43 Weymouth Mews
London W1G 7EQ
T 7580 4412

Dover Street Market [162]
17–18 Dover Street
London W1S 4LT
T 7518 0680
E info@doverstreetmarket.com
W www.doverstreetmarket.com

Dower & Hall [38]
60 Beauchamp Place
London SW3 1NZ
T 7589 8474

E info@dowerandhall.com
W www.dowerandhall.com

Dragana Perisic [91]
30 Cheshire Street
London E2 6EH
T 7739 4484
E info@draganaperisic.com
W www.draganaperisic.com

The Drapers Arms [77]
44 Barnsbury Street
London N1 1ER
T 7619 0348
E info@thedrapersarms.co.uk
W www.thedrapersarms.co.uk

Dreambagsjaguarshoes [94]
34–36 Kingsland Road
London E2 8DA
T 7729 5830
W www.dreambagsjaguarshoes.com

Duchamp [23]
75 Ledbury Road
London W11 2AG
T 7243 3970
E customerservice@duchamp.co.uk
W www.duchamp.co.uk

The Duke [67]
7 Roger Street
London WC1N 2PB
T 7242 7230
E enquiries@dukepub.co.uk
W www.dukepub.co.uk

Duke of Cambridge [77]
30 St Peter's Street
London N1 8JT
T 7359 3066
E duke@dukeorganic.co.uk
W www.sloeberry.co.uk

Dunhill [164]
48 Jermyn Street
London SW1Y 6DL
T 7290 8602
E customer.services@dunhill.com
W www.dunhill.com

The Eagle [138]
159 Farringdon Road
London EC1R 3AL
T 7837 1353

**Ebury Wine Bar
& Restaurant** [37]
139 Ebury Street
London SW1W 9QU
T 7730 5447
E ebury@eburywinebar.co.uk
W www.eburywinebar.co.uk

EC One [51]
41 Exmouth Market
London EC1R 4QL
T 8995 9515
W www.econe.co.uk

Effi Samara [48]
15 Dover Street
London W1S 4RT
T 7409 1300
E info@effi-samara.co.uk
W www.ella1.moonfruit.com

Egg [38]
36 Kinnerton Street
London SW1X 8ES
T 7235 9315
E egg@eggtrading.com
W www.eggtrading.eu

The Electric Cinema [19]
191 Portobello Road
London W11 2ED
T 7908 9696
W www.electriccinema.co.uk

Electricity Showrooms [159]
39A Hoxton Square
London N1 6NN
T 7739 6934
E info@electricityshowrooms.co.uk
W www.electricityshowrooms.co.uk

Eleven Cadogan Gardens [124]
11 Cadogan Gardens
London SW3 2RJ
T 7730 7000
E letterbox@number-eleven.co.uk
W www.number-eleven.co.uk

Eley Kishimoto [168]
27 Greek Street
London W1D 5DF
W www.eleykishimoto.com

The Elk in the Woods [156]
39 Camden Passage
London N1 8EA
T 7226 3535
E info@the-elk-in-the-woods.co.uk
W www.the-elk-in-the-woods.co.uk

Ella Doran [91]
46 Cheshire Street
London E2 6EH
T 7613 0782
E info@elladoran.co.uk
W www.elladoran.co.uk

Emmett London [32]
380 King's Road
London SW3 5UZ
T 7351 7529
E info@emmettshirts.com
W www.emmettlondon.com

Erickson Beamon [37]
38 Elizabeth Street
London SW1W 9NZ
T 7259 0202
E natalie@ericksonbeamon.co.uk
W www.ericksonbeamon.com

Estorick Collection [74]
39A Canonbury Square
London N1 2AN
T 7704 9522
E info@estorickcollection.com
W www.estorickcollection.com

Euphorium Bakery [74]
202 Upper Street
London N1 1RQ
T 7704 6905
W www.euphoriumbakery.com

Eyre Brothers [93]
70 Leonard Street
London EC2A 4QX
T 7613 5346
W www.eyrebrothers.co.uk

Family Tree [79]
53 Exmouth Market
London EC1R 4QL
T 7278 1084
E mail@familytreeshop.co.uk
W www.familytreeshop.co.uk

Fandango [74]
50 Cross Street
London N1 2BA
T 7226 1777

Fashion & Textile Museum [106]
83 Bermondsey Street
London SE1 3XF
T 7407 8664
E info@ftmlondon.org
W www.ftmlondon.org

Fino [62]
33 Charlotte Street
London W1T 1RR
T 7813 8010
E reception@finorestaurant.com
W www.finorestaurant.com

Fiona Knapp [23]
178A Westbourne Grove
London W11 2RH
T 7313 5941
E info@fionaknapp.com
W www.fionaknapp.com

Fish Shop on St John Street [77]
360–362 St John Street
London EC1V 4NR
T 7837 1199
E info@thefishshop.net
W www.thefishshop.net

Flow [20]
1–5 Needham Road
London W11 2RP
T 7243 0782
E info@flowgallery.co.uk
W www.flowgallery.co.uk

The Fox Club London [126]
46 Clarges Street
London W1J 7EF
T 7495 3656
E bethan@foxclublondon.com
W www.foxclublondon.com

Frederick's [77]
106 Camden Passage
London N1 8EG
T 7359 2888
E eat@fredericks.co.uk
W www.fredericks.co.uk

The French House [51]
49 Dean Street
London W1D 5BG
T 7437 2477

Gallery 1930/Susie Cooper Ceramics [174]
18 Church Street
London NW8 8EP
T 7723 1555
E gallery1930@aol.com
W www.susiecooperceramics.com

The Garrison [106]
99 Bermondsey Street
London SE1 3XB
T 7089 9355
E info@thegarrison.co.uk
W www.thegarrison.co.uk

Gary Anderson [61]
36 Chiltern Street
London W1U 7QJ
T 7224 2241
W www.garyanderson.com

Gary Grant Choice Pieces [78]
18 Arlington Way
London EC1R 1UY
T 7713 1122

Geale's [25]
2 Farmer Street
London W8 7SN
T 7727 7528
E info@geales.com
W www.geales.com

Geffrye Museum [94]
Kingsland Road
London E2 3EA
T 7739 9893
E info@geffrye-museum.org.uk
W www.geffrye-museum.org.uk

Geo F. Trumper [44]
9 Curzon Street
London W1J 5HQ
T 7499 1850
E enquiries@trumpers.com
W www.trumpers.com

The George Inn [105]
77 Borough High Street
London SE1 1NH
T 7407 2056
E georgeinn@nationaltrust.org.uk
W www.nationaltrust.org.uk

Get Stuffed [74]
105 Essex Road
London N1 2SL
T 7226 1364
E taxidermy@thegetstuffed.co.uk
W www.thegetstuffed.co.uk

Ghost [25]
36 Ledbury Road
London W11 2AB
T 7229 1057
E info@ghost.co.uk
W www.ghost.co.uk

Gieves & Hawkes [165]
1 Savile Row
London W1S 3JR
T 7434 2001
E gieves@gievesandhawkes.com
W www.gievesandhawkes.com

Gill Wing Shops [74]
182, 190, 194 and 196 Upper Street
London N1 1RQ
T 7359 7697

Gordon's Wine Bar [151]
47 Villiers Street
London WC2N 6NE
T 7930 1408
E simon@gordonswinebar.com
W www.gordonswinebar.com

Great Eastern Dining Rooms [159]
54–56 Great Eastern Street
London EC2A 3QR
T 7613 4545
E greateastern@rickerrestaurants.com
W www.greateasterndining.co.uk

The Grill Room [136]
Dorchester Hotel, 53 Park Lane
London W1K 1QA
T 7629 8888
E info@dorchesterhotel.com
W www.dorchesterhotel.com

Groom [38]
49 Beauchamp Place
London SW3 1NY
T 7581 1248
E info@groomlondon.com
W www.groomlondon.com

The Guinea [46]
30 Bruton Place
London W1J 6NL
T 7499 1210
E guinea@youngs.co.uk
W www.theguinea.co.uk

Hakkasan [133]
8 Hanway Place
London W1T 1HD
T 7907 1888
E mail@hakkasan.com

Handmade & Found [74]
109 Essex Road
London N1 2SL
T 7359 3898
E info@handmadeandfound.co.uk
W www.handmadeandfound.com

Harvie & Hudson [164]
96–97 Jermyn Street
London SW1Y 6JE
T 7839 3578
E info@harvieandhudson.com
W www.harvieandhudson.com

The Havelock Tavern [25]
57 Masbro Road
London W14 0LS
T 7603 5374
E info@thehavelocktavern.co.uk
W www.thehavelocktavern.co.uk

The Haymarket Hotel [122]
1 Suffolk Place
London SW1Y 4BP
T 7470 4000
E haymarket@firmdale.com
W www.firmdale.com

Hayward Gallery [102]
South Bank Centre
Belvedere Road
London SE1 8XX
T 8703 800 400
W www.haywardgallery.org.uk

Hazlitt's [116]
6 Frith Street
London W1D 3JA
T 7434 1771
E reservations@hazlitts.co.uk
W www.hazlittshotel.com

Her House [94]
26 Drysdale Street
London N1 6LS
T 7729 2760
E morag@herhouse.uk.com
W www.herhouse.uk.com

Holly & Lil [106]
103 Bermondsey Street
London SE1 3XB
T 07811 715 452
E collars@hollyandlil.co.uk
W www.hollyandlil.co.uk

Home [93]
100–106 Leonard Street
London EC2A 4RH
T 7684 8618
E mail@homebar.co.uk
W www.homebar.co.uk

Howarth of London [61]
31 Chiltern Street
London W1U 7PN
T 7935 2407
E sales@howarth.uk.com
W www.howarth.uk.com

Hoxton Apprentice [92]
16 Hoxton Square
London N1 6NT
T 7749 2828
W www.hoxtonapprentice.com

**Hoxton Square Bar
& Kitchen** [159]
2–4 Hoxton Square
London N1 6NU
T 7613 0709

The Hoxton Urban Lodge [112]
81 Great Eastern Street
London EC2A 3HU
T 7550 1000
E info@hoxtonhotels.com
W www.hoxtonhotels.com

Inn the Park [149]
St James's Park
London SW1A 2BJ
T 7451 9999
E info@innthepark.com
W www.innthepark.com

J. Floris [164]
89 Jermyn Street
London SW1Y 6JH
T 0845 702 3239
E fragrance@florislondon.com
W www.florislondon.com

J. Sheekey [50]
28–32 St Martin's Court
London WC2N 4AL
T 7240 2565
W www.j-sheekey.co.uk

The Jacksons [20]
5 All Saints Road
London W11 1HA
T 7792 8336
E becki@thejacksons.co.uk
W www.thejacksons.co.uk

James Smith & Sons [66]
53 New Oxford Street
London WC1A 1BL
T 7836 4731
W www.james-smith.co.uk

Jess James [51]
3 Newburgh Street
London W1F 7RE
T 7437 0199
E jess@jessjames.com
W www.jessjames.com

John Lobb [166]
88 Jermyn Street
London SW1Y 6JD
T 7930 8089
E shop@johnlobb.co.uk
W www.johnlobb.co.uk

John Rocha [48]
15A Dover Street
London W1S 4LR
T 7495 2233
E shop@johnrocha.ie
W www.johnrocha.ie

Julie's [18]
135 Portland Road
London W11 4LW
T 7229 8331
E info@juliesrestaurant.com
W www.juliesrestaurant.com

Junky [88]
12 Dray Walk
91 Brick Lane

London E1 6RF
T 7247 1883
E junky.styling@virgin.net
W www.junkystyling.co.uk

Kilgour [165]
8 Savile Row
London W1S 3PE
T 7734 6905
E enquiries@kilgour.eu
W www.kilgour.eu

The King's Head [74]
115 Upper Street
London N1 1QN
T 7226 1916
E info@kingsheadtheatre.org
W www.kingsheadtheatre.org

Koh Samui [55]
65–67 Monmouth Street
London WC2H 9DJ
T 7240 4280

Konstam [73]
2 Acton Street
London WC1X 9NA
T 7833 5040
E princealbert@konstam.co.uk
W www.konstam.co.uk

L. Cornelissen & Son [66]
105 Great Russell Street
London WC1B 3RY
T 7636 1045
E info@cornelissen.co.uk
W www.cornelissen.co.uk

Labour and Wait [91]
18 Cheshire Street
London E2 6EH
T 7729 6253
E info@labourandwait.co.uk
W www.labourandwait.co.uk

Lara Bohinc 107 [170]
51 Hoxton Square
London N1 6PB
T 7684 1465
E info@larabohinc.com
W www.larabohinc.com

The Ledbury [23]
127 Ledbury Road
London W11 2AQ
T 7792 9090
E info@theledbury.com
W www.theledbury.com

Leighton House Museum [25]
12 Holland Park Road
London W14 8LZ
T 7602 3316
E leightonhousemuseum@
   rbkc.gov.uk
W www.rbkc.gov.uk/
   leightonhousemuseum

Leila's Shop [91]
17 Calvert Avenue
London E2 7JP
T 7729 9789

Lesley Craze Gallery [81]
33–35A Clerkenwell Green
London EC1R 0DU
T 7608 0393
E jewellery@lesleycrazegallery.co.uk
W www.lesleycrazegallery.co.uk

Lindsay House [135]
21 Romilly Street
London W1D 5AF
T 7439 0450

E richardcorrigan@
   linsayhouse.co.uk
W www.lindsayhouse.co.uk

Liquid [159]
8 Pitfield Street
London N1 6HA
T 7729 0082

London Eye [100]
Jubilee Gardens
London SE1 7PB
T 0870 990 8883
E customer.services@
   ba-londoneye.com
W www.londoneye.com

London Harpsichord Centre [61]
14 Chiltern Street
London W1U 7PY
T 7935 0789

London Review Bookshop [65]
14 Bury Place
London WC1A 2JL
T 7269 9030
E books@lrbshop.co.uk
W www.lrbshop.co.uk

London Silver Vaults [65]
53–64 Chancery Lane
London WC2A 1QS
T 7242 3844
W www.thesilvervaults.com

Lulu Guinness [35]
3 Ellis Street
London SW1X 9AL
T 7823 4828
E ellisstreet@luluguinness.com
W www.luluguinness.com

Magdalen Restaurant [105]
152 Tooley Street
London SE1 2TU
T 7403 1342
E info@magdalenrestaurant.co.uk
W www.magdalenrestaurant.co.uk

Magma [55]
8 Earlham Street
London WC2H 9RY
T 7240 8498
E enquiries@magmabooks.com
W www.magmabooks.com

The Main House [128]
6 Colville Road
London W11 2BP
T 7221 9691
E caroline@themainhouse.co.uk
W www.themainhouse.co.uk

The Mall [77]
359 Upper Street
London N1 0PD
T 7823 3900
E info@themallantiques.co.uk
W www.mallantiques.co.uk

Manolo Blahník [32]
49–51 Old Church Street
London SW3 5BS
T 7352 8622
W www.manoloblahnik.com

The Map House [38]
54 Beauchamp Place
London SW3 1NY
T 7589 4325
E maps@themaphouse.com
W www.themaphouse.com

Mar Mar [91]
16 Cheshire Street
London E2 6EH
T 7729 1494
E office@marmarco.com
W www.marmarco.com

Marcus Campbell Art Books [102]
43 Holland Street
London SE1 9JR
T 7261 0111
E info@marcuscampbell.co.uk
W www.marcuscampbell.co.uk

Margaret Howell [163]
34 Wigmore Street
London W1U 2RS
T 7009 9006
E wigmorestreet@
   margarethowell.co.uk
W www.margarethowell.co.uk

The Marquess Tavern [77]
32 Canonbury Street
London N1 2TB
T 7354 2975
E info@marquesstavern.co.uk
W www.marquesstavern.co.uk

Marx Memorial Library [81]
37A Clerkenwell Green
London EC1R 0DU
T 7253 1485
E marxlibrary@britishlibrary.net
W www.marx-memorial-library.org

Mary Moore [18]
5 Clarendon Cross
London W11 4AP
T 7229 5678
E info@marymoorevintage.com
W www.marymoorevintage.com

Matthew Williamson [47]
28 Bruton Street
London W1J 6QH
T 7629 6200
E aitzi@matthewwilliamson.co.uk
W www.matthewwilliamson.co.uk

Medcalf [79]
40 Exmouth Market
London EC1R 4QE
T 7833 3533
E mail@medcalfbar.co.uk
W www.medcalfbar.co.uk

Medicine Bar [159]
89 Great Eastern Street
London EC2A 3HX
T 7739 5173
E shoreditch@medicinebar.net
W www.medicinebar.net

Melt [175]
59 Ledbury Road
London W11 2AA
T 7727 5030
E kitchen@meltchocolates.com
W www.meltchocolates.com

Miller Harris [20]
14 Needham Road
London W11 2RP
T 7221 1545
E info@millerharris.com
W www.millerharris.com

Mint [62]
70 Wigmore Street
London W1U 2SF
T 7224 4406
E info@mintshop.co.uk

W www.mintshop.co.uk

Monmouth Coffee House [55]
27 Monmouth Street
London WC2H 9EU
T 7379 3516
E beans@monmouthcoffee.co.uk
W www.monmouthcoffee.co.uk

Moro [79]
34–36 Exmouth Market
London EC1R 4QE
T 7833 8336
E info@moro.co.uk
W www.moro.co.uk

Murdock [91]
340 Old Street
London EC1V 9DS
T 7729 2288
E info@murdocklondon.com
W www.murdocklondon.com

Natéclo [17]
14 Portobello Green
281 Portobello Road
London W10 5TZ
T 7814 025 796

National Theatre [102]
South Bank Centre
London SE1 9PX
T 7452 3000
E info@nationaltheatre.org.uk
W www.nationaltheatre.org.uk

Neal's Yard Dairy [55]
17 Shorts Gardens
London WC2H 9UP
T 7240 5700
E coventgarden@
   nealsyarddairy.co.uk
W www.nealsyarddairy.co.uk/

Neal's Yard Remedies [55]
15 Neal's Yard
London WC2H 9DP
T 7379 7222
E cgarden@nealsyardremedies.co.uk
W www.nealsyardremedies.com

Neisha Crosland [32]
8 Elystan Street
London SW3 3NS
T 7584 7988
E elystanstreet@
   neishacrosland.com
W www.neishacrosland.com

New Tayyabs [88]
83–89 Fieldgate Street
London E1 1JU
T 7247 6400
E info@tayyabs.co.uk
W www.tayyabs.co.uk

The Old Queen's Head [74]
44 Essex Road
London N1 8LN
T 7354 9993
E shelley@theoldqueenshead.com
W www.theoldqueenshead.com

The Old Truman Brewery [88]
91 Brick Lane
London E1 6QL
T 7770 6100
E events@trumanbrewery.com
W www.trumanbrewery.com

The Old Curiosity Shop [55]
13–14 Portsmouth Street
London WC2A 2ES
T 7405 9891

E info@curiosityuk.com
W www.curiosityuk.com

Old Vic Theatre [105]
The Cut
London SE1 8NB
T 0870 060 6628
E ovtcadmin@oldvictheatre.com
W www.oldvictheatre.com

Orla Kiely [53]
31 Monmouth Street
London WC2H 9DD
T 7240 4022
E shop@orlakiely.com
W www.orlakiely.com

Ormonde Jayne [167]
The Royal Arcade
28 Old Bond Street
London W1S 4SL
T 7499 1100
E sales@ormondejayne.com
W www.ormondejayne.com

Oxo Tower [100]
Bargehouse Street
London SE1 9PH
T 7803 3888
W www.oxotower.co.uk

Palette London [77]
21 Canonbury Lane
London N1 2AS
T 7288 7428
E sales@palette-london.com
W www.palette-london.com

Passione [62]
10 Charlotte Street
London W1T 2LT
T 7636 2833
E liz@passione.co.uk
W www.passione.co.uk

Paul Smith [166]
40–44 Floral Street
London WC2E 9DS
T 7379 7133

Paul Smith Curiosity Shop [48]
9 Albemarle Street
London W1S 4HH
T 7495 4708
W www.paulsmith.co.uk

Philip Somerville [61]
38 Chiltern Street
London W1U 7QL
T 7224 1517
E info@philipsomerville.com
W www.philipsomerville.com

Philip Treacy [171]
69 Elizabeth Street
London SW1W 9PJ
T 7824 8787
W www.philiptreacy.co.uk

Philmore Clague [17]
25 Portobello Green
281 Portobello Road
London W10 5TZ
T 8964 1121
E philmoreclague@hotmail.com

Pied à Terre [62]
34 Charlotte Street
London W1T 2NH
T 7636 1178
E info@pied-a-terre.co.uk
W www.pied-a-terre.co.uk

Pippa Small [170]
11 Colville Mews
London W11 2DA
T 7792 1292
E info@pippasmall.com
W www.pippasmall.com

Poetry Café [53]
22 Betterton Street
London WC2H 9BX
T 7420 9887
E poetrycafe@poetrysociety.org.uk
W www.poetrysociety.org.uk

The Portrait Restaurant [150]
The National Portrait Gallery
St Martin's Place
London WC2H 0HE
T 7312 2490
W www.npg.org.uk

Preen [169]
5 Portobello Green
281 Portobello Road
London W10 5TZ
T 8968 1542

Quality Chop House [78]
92–94 Farringdon Raod
London EC1R 3EA
T 7837 5093
E enquiries@
   qualitychophouse.co.uk
W www.qualitychophouse.co.uk

Rachel Riley [37]
14 Pont Street
London SW1X 9EN
T 7259 5969
E enquiries@rachelriley.co.uk
W www.rachelriley.com

Ragam [65]
57 Cleveland Street
London W1T 4JN
T 7636 9098

Rasa Samudra [62]
5 Charlotte Street
London W1T 1RE
T 7637 0222
W www.rasarestaurants.com

Rasoi Vineet Bhatia [143]
10 Lincoln Street
London SW3 2TS
T 7225 1881
E info@rasarestaurants.com
W www.vineetbhatia.com

Red Fort [143]
77 Dean Street
London W1D 3SH
T 7437 2525
E info@redfort.co.uk
W www.redfort.co.uk

Rellik [169]
8 Golborne Road
London W10 5NW
T 8962 0089
W www.relliklondon.co.uk

Richard James [165]
29 Savile Row
London W1S 2EY
T 7434 0605
E mail@richardjames.co.uk
W www.richardjames.co.uk

Roast [106]
The Floral Hall, Borough Market
Stoney Street
London, SE1 1TL

T 7940 1300
E feedback@roast-restaurant.com
W www.roast-restaurant.com

Rochelle Canteen [91]
Rochelle School, Arnold Circus
London E2 7ES
T 7729 5677
E info@arnoldandhenderson.com
W www.arnoldandhenderson.com

Roka [62]
37 Charlotte Street
London W1T 1RR
T 7580 6464
E info@rokarestaurant.com
W www.rokarestaurant.com

Rokit [53]
42 Shelton Street
London WC2 9HZ
T 7836 6547
E info@rokit.co.uk
W www.rokit.co.uk

Ronnie Scott's [52]
47 Frith Street
London W1D 4HT
T 7439 0747
E ronniescotts@ronniescotts.co.uk
W www.ronniescotts.co.uk

The Rookery [120]
Peter's Lane, Cowcross Street
London EC1M 6DS
T 7336 0931
E reservations@rookery.co.uk
W www.rookery.co.uk

Ross+Bute [23]
57 Ledbury Road
London W11 2AA
T 7727 2348
E shop@anonymousclothing.com
W www.anonymousclothing.com

Rough Trade [88]
East Dray Walk
91 Brick Lane
London E1 6QL
T 7392 7788
E enquiries@roughtrade.com
W www.roughtrade.com

Royal Festival Hall [102]
South Bank Centre
London SE1 8XX
T 0871 663 2500
W www.southbankcentre.co.uk

**Royal Institute of British
Architects** [62]
66 Portland Place
London W1B 1AD
T 7580 5533
E info@inst.riba.org
W www.architecture.com

Ruby Lounge [157]
33 Caledonian Road
London N1 9BU
T 7689 1370
E kingsx@ruby.uk.com
W www.ruby.uk.com

Rules [134]
35 Maiden Lane
London WC2E 7LB
T 7836 5314
E info@rules.co.uk
W www.rules.co.uk

Rupert Sanderson [46]
33 Bruton Place

London W1J 6NP
T 7491 2427
E info@rupertsanderson.co.uk
W www.rupertsanderson.co.uk

S&M Café [74]
4–6 Essex Road
London N1 8LN
T 7359 5361
E anne@sandmcafe.co.uk
W www.sandmcafe.co.uk

Sadler's Wells [77]
Rosebery Avenue
London EC1R 4TN
T 7863 8198
E reception@sadlerswells.com
W www.sadlerswells.com

St Alban [133]
4–12 Regent Street
London SW1Y 4PE
T 7499 8558
E info@stalban.net
W www.stalban.net

St Bartholomew the Great [80]
West Smithfield
London EC1A 7JQ
T 7606 5171
E admin@greatstbarts.com
W www.greatstbarts.com

St John [144]
26 St John Street
London EC1M 4AY
T 7251 0848
W www.stjohnrestaurant.co.uk

St Pancras Station [73]
Pancras Road
London NW1 2QP
W www.stpancras.com

St Stephen Walbrook [86]
39 Walbrook
London EC4N 8BN
T 7626 9000
W www.ststephenwalbrook.net

Sasti [17]
8 Portobello Green
281 Portobello Road
London W10 5TY
T 8960 1125
W www.sasti.co.uk

The Scarsdale Tavern [25]
23A Edwardes Square
London W8 6HE
T 7937 1811

Scott's [142]
20 Mount Street
London W1K 2HE
T 7495 7309

Serpentine Gallery [30]
Kensington Gardens
London W2 3XA
T 7402 6075
E information@
serpentinegallery.org
W www.serpentinegallery.org

Shakespeare's Globe [102]
21 New Globe Walk
London SE1 9DT
T 7902 1409
E info@shakespearesglobe.com
W www.shakespeares-globe.org

Sir John Soane's Museum [67]
13 Lincoln's Inn Fields

London WC2A 3BP
T 7405 2107
W www.soane.org

Sketch [140]
9 Conduit Street
London W1S 2XG
T 0870 777 4488
W www.sketch.uk.com

Skylon Restaurant [102]
South Bank Centre
Belvedere Road
London SE1 8XX
T 7654 7800
W www.skylonrestaurant.co.uk

Smiths of Smithfield [81]
67–77 Charterhouse Street
London EC1M 6HJ
T 7251 7950
E reservations@
smithsofsmithfield.co.uk
W www.smithsofsmithfield.co.uk

Smithy's [153]
15–17 Leeke Street
London WC1X 9HZ
T 7278 5949

The Social [157]
5 Little Portland Street
London W1W 7JD
T 7636 4992
W www.thesocial.com

Solange Azagury-Partridge [171]
187 Westbourne Grove
London W11 2SB
T 7792 0197
E info@solange.info
W www.
solangeazagurypartridge.com

Somerset House [55]
Strand
London WC2R 1LA
T 7845 4600
E info@somerset-house.org.uk
W www.somerset-house.org.uk

South Bank Centre [102]
Belvedere Road
London SE1 8XX
T 0871 663 2500
E customer@southbankcentre.co.uk
W www.sbc.org.uk

Southwark Cathedral [105]
Montague Close
London SE1 9DA
T 7367 6700
E cathedral@
southwark.anglican.org
W www.southwark.anglican.org/
cathedral/

The Spice Shop [20]
1 Blenheim Crescent
London W11 2EE
T 7221 4448
E enquiries@thespiceshop.co.uk
W www.thespiceshop.co.uk

Spitalfields Market [91]
Commercial Street
London E1
W www.spitalfields.org.uk

The Square Pie Company [91]
Spitalfields Market, 16 Horner Square
London E1 2600
T 7377 1114
E spitalfields@squarepie.com

W www.squarepie.com

Start [94]
42–44 Rivington Street
(womenswear)
London EC2A 3BN
T 7729 3334
59 Rivington Street (menswear)
London EC2A 3QQ
T 7739 3636
E info@start-london.com
W www.start-london.com

Stella McCartney [173]
30 Bruton Street
London W1J 6LG
T 7518 3100
E london@stellamccartney.com
W www.stellamccartney.com

Stephen Einhorn [74]
210 Upper Street
London N1 1RL
T 7359 4977
E info@stepheneinhorn.co.uk
W www.stepheneinhorn.co.uk

Susy Harper [77]
35 Camden Passage
London N1 8EA
T 7704 0688
E shop@susyharper.co.uk
W www.susyharper.co.uk

Sweetings [87]
39 Queen Victoria Street
London EC4N 4SF
T 7248 3062

Tadema Gallery [77]
10 Charlton Place
London N1 8AJ
T 7359 1055
E info@tademagallery.com
W www.tademagallery.com

Le Taj [88]
96 Brick Lane
London E1 6RL
T 7247 0733
E info@letaj.co.uk
W www.letaj.co.uk

Target Gallery [65]
7 Windmill Street
London W1T 2JE
T 7636 6295

Tate Modern [101]
Bankside
London SE1 9TG
T 7887 8888
E visiting.modern@tate.org.uk
W www.tate.org.uk/modern

Tate-to-Tate Boat Service [102]
Thames Clippers
T 7887 8888
E web@thamesclippers.com
W www.thamesclippers.com

Tatty Devine [88]
236 Brick Lane
London E2 7EB
T 7739 9191
E info@tattydevine.com
W www.tattydevine.com

Tea Palace [148]
175 Westbourne Grove
London W11 2SB
T 7727 2600
E info@teapalace.co.uk
W www.teapalace.com

The Thomas Cubitt [37]
44 Elizabeth Street
London SW1W 9PA
T 7730 6060
E reservations@
thethomascubitt.co.uk
W www.thethomascubitt.co.uk

Thorsten van Elten [65]
22 Warren Street
London W1T 5LU
T 7388 8008
E info@thorstenvanelten.com
W www.thorstenvanelten.com

Timorous Beasties [78]
46 Amwell Street
London EC1R 1XS
T 7833 5010
E london@timorousbeasties.com
W www.timorousbeasties.com

Timothy Everest [44]
35 Bruton Place
London W1J 6NS
T 7629 6236
E brutonplace@
timothyeverest.co.uk
W www.timothyeverest.co.uk

Tom Aikens [145]
43 Elystan Street
London SW3 3NT
T 7584 2003
E info@tomaikens.co.uk
W www.tomaikens.co.uk

Tom's Kitchen [31]
27 Cale Street
London SW3 3QP
T 7349 0202
E info@tomskitchen.co.uk
W www.tomskitchen.co.uk

Townhouse [38]
31 Beauchamp Place
London SW3 1NU
T 0870 242 1428
E info@lab-townhouse.com
W www.lab-townhouse.com

Tracey Boyd's House [37]
42 Elizabeth Street
London SW1W 9NZ
T 7730 3939
E adrian@traceyboyd.com
W www.traceyboyd.com

Trailer Happiness [158]
177 Portobello Road
London W11 2DY
T 7727 2700
E bookings@trailerh.com
W www.trailerhappiness.co.uk

Les Trois Garçons [92]
1 Club Row
London E1 6JX
T 7613 1924
E info@lestroisgarcons.com
W www.lestroisgarcpns.com

Turnbull & Asser [164]
71–72 Jermyn Street
London SW1Y 6PF
T 7808 3000
W www.turnbullandasser.com

Twenty8Twelve [23]
172 Westbourne Grove
London W11 2RW
T 7221 9287
E info@twenty8twelve.com
W www.twenty8twelve.com

Twentytwentyone [74]
274 Upper Street
London N1 2UA
T 7288 1996
E shop@twentytwentyone.com
W www.twentytwentyone.com

Umu [132]
14–16 Bruton Place
London W1J 6LX
T 7499 8881
W www.umurestaurant.com

Unto This Last [88]
230 Brick Lane
London E2 7EB
T 7613 0882
E comments@untothislast.co.uk
W www.untothislast.co.uk

V.V. Rouleaux [35]
54 Sloane Square
London SW1W 8AX
T 7730 3125
E sloane@vvrouleaux.com
W www.vvrouleaux.com

Vertigo42 [150]
Tower 42, 25 Old Broad Street
London EC2N 1HQ
T 7877 7842
E privateevents@vertigo42.co.uk
W www.vertigo42.co.uk

Vessel [19]
114 Kensington Park Road
London W11 2PW
T 7727 8001
E info@vesselgallery.com
W www.vesselgallery.com

Vibe Bar [88]
The Old Truman Brewery
91 Brick Lane
London E1 6QL
T 7426 0491
E info@vibe-bar.co.uk
W www.vibe-bar.co.uk

Victoria & Albert Museum [30]
Cromwell Road
London SW7 2RL
T 7942 2000
E vanda@vam.ac.uk
W www.vam.ac.uk

Viet Hoa [94]
70–72 Kingsland Road
London E2 8DP
T 7729 8293

Village East [106]
171–173 Bermondsey Street
London SE1 3UW
T 7357 6082
E info@villageeast.co.uk
W www.villageeast.co.uk

Villandry [62]
170 Great Portland Street
London W1W 5QB
T 7631 3131
E contactus@villandry.com
W www.villandry.com

Vinopolis [105]
1 Bank End
London SE1 9BU
T 0870 241 4040
E sales@vinopolis.co.uk
W www.vinopolis.co.uk

The Vintage House [50]
42 Old Compton Street

London W1D 4LR
T 7437 5112
E info@sohowhisky.com
W www.sohowhisky.com

Virginia [18]
98 Portland Road
Clarendon Cross
London W11 4LQ
T 7727 9908

Wall [25]
1 Denbigh Road
London W11 2SJ
T 7243 4623
E nottinghill.wall@btconnect.com
W www.wall-london.com

The Wallace Collection [61]
Hertford House, Manchester Square
London W1U 3BN
T 7563 9500
E visiting@wallacecollection.org
W www.wallacecollection.org

Wallace Sewell [78]
24 Lloyd Baker Street
London WC1X 9AZ
T 7833 2995
E studio@wallacesewell.com
W www.wallacesewell.com

The Westbourne [20]
101 Westbourne Park Villas
London W2 5ED
T 7221 1332
W www.thewestbourne.com

White Cube [94]
48 Hoxton Square
London N1 6PB
T 7930 5373
E enquiries@whitecube.com
W www.whitecube.com

Whitechapel Art Gallery [86]
80–82 Whitechapel High Street
London E1 7QX
T 7522 7878
E info@whitechapel.org
W www.whitechapel.org

Wild Honey [44]
2 St George Street
London W1S 2FB
T 7758 9160

William Hunt [165]
41 Savile Row
London W1X 1AG
T 7439 1921
E williamhunt@btconnect.com
W www.williamhunt-savilerow.com

William Yeoward Crystal [32]
270 King's Road
London SW3 5AW
T 7349 7828
E store@williamyeoward.com
W www.williamyeoward.com

Windsor Castle [154]
114 Campden Hill Road
London W8 7AR
T 7243 9551

The Wolseley [136]
160 Piccadilly
London W1J 9EB
T 7499 6996
W www.thewolseley.com

Wright Brothers [106]
Borough Market, 11 Stoney Street

London SE1 9AD
T 7403 9554
E info@wrightbros.eu.com
W www.wrightbros.eu.com

Yauatcha [141]
15 Broadwick Street
London W1F 0DL
T 7494 8888

Ye Olde Mitre Tavern [152]
1 Ely Court
London EC1N 6SJ
T 7405 4751

Zarvis [17]
4 Portobello Green
281 Portobello Road
London W10 5TZ
T 8968 5435
E v.zarvis@virgin.net
W www.zarvis.com

The Zetter [114]
St John's Square
86–88 Clerkenwell Road
London EC1M 5RJ
T 7324 4444
E info@thezetter.com
W www.thezetter.com

BRIGHTON [178]
*Direct trains to Brighton leave
approximately every half hour from
King's Cross Thameslink, London
Bridge (1 hour and 20 minutes) and
Victoria stations (50 minutes). (From
London call 0845 748 4950 or check
www.railtrack.co.uk for specific times.)
Both hotels and most destinations in
Brighton are walking distance from the
station; taxis are plentiful.*

Blanch House
17 Atlingworth Street
Brighton
East Sussex BN2 1PL
T 01273 603 504
E info@blanchhouse.co.uk
W www.blanchhouse.co.uk
Rooms from £125

Hotel Pelirocco
10 Regency Square
Brighton
East Sussex BN1 2FG
T 01273 327 055
E info@hotelpelirocco.co.uk
W www.hotelpelirocco.co.uk
Rooms from £100

The Royal Pavilion
Brighton
East Sussex BN1 1EE
T 01273 290 900
E royalpavilion@
brighton-hove.gov.uk
W www.royalpavilion.org.uk

BATH [180]
*Fast trains to Bath leave every hour
(from London call 0845 748 4950 or
check www.railtrack.co.uk for specific
times); from Paddington Station the
trip takes 1 hour and 20 minutes.
Babington House is approximately
12 miles from Bath. The easiest way
of reaching the hotel is by taxi; the fare
is £25 to £30.*

Babington House
Babington, near Frome
Somerset BA11 3RW

T 01373 812 266
E enquiries@babingtonhouse.co.uk
W www.babingtonhouse.co.uk
Rooms from £210

BRAY-ON-THAMES [182]
*The 30- to 40-minute train journey to
Maidenhead leaves approximately every
half hour from Paddington Station
(from London call 0845 748 4950 or
check www.railtrack.co.uk for specific
times). Take a taxi from Maidenhead
station to Bray High Street or directly to
any of the destinations below; fares are
about £10.*

The Waterside Inn
Ferry Road
Bray-on-Thames
Berkshire SL6 2AT
T 01628 620 691
E reservations@waterside-inn.co.uk
W www.waterside-inn.co.uk
Rooms from £160

The Fat Duck
High Street
Bray-on-Thames
Berkshire SL6 2AQ
T 01628 580 333
W www.fatduck.co.uk

The Hind's Head
The High Street
Bray-on-Thames
Berkshire
T 01628 626 151
W www.thehindsheadhotel.com

Monkey Island Hotel
Bray-on-Thames
Berkshire SL6 2EE
T 01628 623 400
E reception@monkeyisland.co.uk
W www.methotels.com/
monkeyisland
Rooms from £200

GRAVETYE MANOR [184]
*Take the 50-minute train ride from
London Victoria to East Grinstead;
trains leave every half hour (from
London call 08457 48 49 50 or check
www.railtrack.co.uk for specific times).
From the station, take a taxi to the
hotel; the fare is about £15.*

Gravetye Manor
near East Grinstead
West Sussex RH19 4LJ
T 01342 810 567
E info@gravetyemanor.co.uk
W www.gravetyemanor.co.uk
Rooms from £210